MORE FROM THE SAGER GROUP

The Stacks Reader Series

The Cheerleaders: A True Story by E. Jean Carroll

An American Family: A True Story by Daniel Voll

Flesh and Blood: A True Story by Peter Richmond

An Accidental Martyr: A True Story by Chip Brown

Death of a Playmate: A True Story by Teresa Carpenter

The Detective: And Other True Stories by Walt Harrington

Soldiers in the Army of God: A True Story by Daniel Voll

Original Gangster: A True Story by Paul Solotaroff

The Dreamer Deceiver: A True Story by Ivan Solotaroff

Mary in the Lavender Pumps: A True Story by Joyce Wadler

General Interest

The Stories We Tell: Classic True Tales by America's Greatest Women Journalists

New Stories We Tell: True Tales by America's New Generation of Great Women Journalists

Newswomen: Twenty-five Years of Front-Page Journalism

The Devil & John Holmes: And Other True Stories by Mike Sager

Lifeboat No. 8: Surviving the Titanic by Elizabeth Kaye

Stopping the Road: The Campaign Against a Trans-Sierra Highway by Jack Fisher

Notes from the Road: A Filmmaker's Journey through American Music by Robert Mugge

What Makes Sammy Jr. Run?: Classic Celebrity Journalism Volume 1, edited by Alex Belth

Secrets of Ash: A Novel of War, Brotherhood, and Going Home Again by Josh Green

MORE FROM
JOHN H. RICHARDSON

Nonfiction

Not Guilty by Reason of Afghanistan: And Other True Stories

In The Little World: A True Story of Dwarves, Love and Trouble

My Father The Spy: An Investigative Memoir

Fiction

The Viper's Club, a novel

SING SING FOLLIES

(A MAXIMUM-SECURITY COMEDY):

AND OTHER TRUE STORIES

JOHN H. RICHARDSON

Cover design and cover art by Sonny and Biddy (SonnyandBiddy.com)
Interior design by Siori Kitajima (PatternBased.com)

Cataloging-in-Publication data for this book
is available from the Library of Congress.
ISBN-13:
eBook: 978-1-958861-39-4
Paperback: 978-1-958861-40-0

Published by The Sager Group LLC
(TheSagerGroup.net)

SING SING FOLLIES

(A MAXIMUM-SECURITY COMEDY):

AND OTHER TRUE STORIES

JOHN H. RICHARDSON

THE SAGER GROUP

Artifex Te Adiuva

CONTENTS

At Sing Sing, the infamous, Gothic maximum-security prison on the Hudson River in New York, some of the incarcerated pass their time and slay inner demons performing theater—in this case a silly slapstick comedy about pirates, gladiators, and mummies on a wacky journey through time. Now a major motion picture, based on the article, starring Colman Domingo. "I've always believed no one should be judged by their worst act," he says. "It's just about, how do we get better?"

JFK praised him. David Halberstam scorned him. The CIA consumed him. Rising out of World War II military intelligence operations, John H. Richardson became the consummate cold warrior, one of the elite CIA station chiefs dispatched to the hottest global hot spots. Along with him, he brought a wife and one very un-CIA-like child of the sixties—his only son, the author.

The story you are about to read is true. Maybe. It involves a fugitive heiress, money, one very real gun, and layer upon layer of internet intimacy and digital deception. It's a mystery that takes place at the edge of technology, and a glimpse of the future we now inhabit—the birth throes of our uncertain world.

On Monday, Michael Brown Sr. will be attending the funeral of his son, who was gunned down by a police officer in Ferguson, Missouri and left bleeding in the street for more than four hours. Amidst the tumult of demonstrations, he's calling for the protesters to be peaceful. His wife tells him, "You can't call for peace looking like you want to hurt somebody." The problem is, he does.

In 2014, the Pink House is the last clinic in Mississippi where a woman can get an abortion, and the state is trying to shut it down—a goal finally achieved when Mississippi banned almost all abortions in 2022. Meet the abortion doctor who is also a Christian raised in the South. He's on a mission from his own personal God.

When you look at the grim facts of climate change day after day for a living, immersing yourself in emission rates, melting ice, rising water, drought, and famine, a good night's sleep can be hard to come by.

In the decades since his last deadly act of ecoterrorism, the Unabomber has become an unlikely prophet to a whole new generation of young acolytes. And what does Ted Kaczynski say? "The political situation is complex and could be discussed endlessly," he tells me, "but for now I will only say this — the current political turmoil provides an environment in which a revolutionary movement should be able to gain a foothold."

INTRODUCTION

ight years ago, I found my way to John's story, *Sing Sing Follies*, quite unexpectedly. I was producing a short documentary inside a maximum-security prison in Kansas. It was my first time ever behind the walls. On a tour of the facility, I passed by a cell and saw something that stopped me in my tracks. . . a young man raising a rescue dog inside of his cell. In that moment, all my expectations about prison and incarcerated people were upended, most of those expectations built by the movies I had grown up watching. And here I was, immediately aware of the healing that was happening in both directions, between this man and animal, that contradicted every stereotype I had been conditioned to believe. I was desperate to know if there were any other programs out there that were doing things differently in prison.

In the hotel that night, I literally typed into Google "who is doing things differently in prison." Near the top of the search field was this theater program in New York, Rehabilitation Through The Arts (RTA). I clicked on the website and started reading. Founded at Sing Sing, the program had been covered in all the major press. They had staged many of the classics over the years from Shakespeare to *On The Waterfront and A Few Good Men*. But then I came across John's article in *Esquire* about the production of one of the only originals they had done inside, a time-traveling musical comedy called *Breakin' the Mummy's Code* written by Brent Buell, and I knew from the first line of his piece that I had to make this movie. Performed for two nights only at Sing Sing, it had pirate ships and Roman gladiators and the black plague. It had musical numbers and rap numbers, and a Hamlet soliloquy.

But what grabbed me so fiercely was the tone of this article, the way John observed and rendered this world. Capturing the intense joy of this production, juxtaposed with the inherent darkness of this setting felt like life to me. Sometimes this duality exists between words in the same sentence. It felt like an invitation that was personally addressed to me.

I wrote John that night. It didn't take long for us to lock arms. And he trusted the process across six years of development. Every time I came back to renew the rights he would always tell me that this was my movie to make. He stood by me. I'll never forget how his belief in me felt then.

John writes in the article about "the ancient idea that literature and art are an essential part of person's moral education." I couldn't agree more. I've seen for myself the power of this through RTA, first as I met the alumni of the program who were home from Sing Sing and featured in this story, and later as a volunteer within the program, teaching film acting in the program at Greenhaven maximum-security prison in New York.

Proximity and time with these men have also been just as instrumental to my moral education as the art itself we were making. And it is across the years, now looking back on this piece, that there are few elements of this article that are worth contextualizing with what I've learned in relationship with the subjects of it. The first is that against John's wishes, the editors at *Esquire* chose to publish the crimes of each man next to their name and photo. I learned later that this was a source of a lot of pain for the men. The article itself possessed such nuance and rich color, showing the fullness of humanity, only to turn a page and be defined once again by their crimes. As Clarence "Divine Eye" Maclin has said often, "We are more than the sum of our worst mistakes. We have more to offer." The second is how language itself has evolved since the publication of this story. There is a growing movement, of which I subscribe, to use people-first language when describing individuals who are incarcerated and no longer using words such as "inmate" or "convict" to describe them. Inmate connotes an identity, where using instead "incarcerated person" literally acknowledges their personhood and places them in a situation versus an all-encompassing label. I like to think it doesn't dismiss where they are and, at the same time, opens doorways for us to access and understand the many dimensions of who they are, and who they can become.

After all these years, we made the movie. It's called *Sing Sing*. We made it alongside many of the alumni of this program, who starred in *Breakin' the Mummy's Code* in 2005. I'm writing this introduction on a flight to New York, where tomorrow we will premiere the film to incarcerated men inside Sing Sing itself, on the same stage where this play was first performed almost twenty years ago. I'll be sitting in the crowd where John once sat with his notebook as the audience showered these artists on stage with applause.

Time is a circle.

I can't wait for you to read this article. I imagine you'll laugh out loud. And you'll come across moments that cut to the bone. This piece is short but packs so much might. I hope it thrills and confounds and inspires you just like it did me that night in my hotel room in Kansas, eight years ago, where in the glow of my laptop I smiled through the tears on my face as I read.

—Greg Kwedar
co-writer, director, and producer of *Sing Sing*

SING SING FOLLIES

(A MAXIMUM- SECURITY COMEDY)

At Sing Sing, the infamous, Gothic maximum-security prison on the Hudson River in New York, some of the incarcerated pass their time and slay inner demons performing theater—in this case a silly slapstick comedy about pirates, gladiators, and mummies on a wacky journey through time. Now a major motion picture, based on the article, stars Colman Domingo. "I've always believed no one should be judged by their worst act," he says. "It's just about, how do we get better?"

S mack in the middle of Sing Sing, the old Gothic prison on the Hudson River—maximum security, with massive gray walls and octagonal watchtowers with snipers in them— Dap stands in front of a blackboard. He has an easy grin and a haircut so tight, it's like paint. "Do you want it like Marilyn Monroe?" he asks.

He says this to Brent Buell, a fifty-eight-year-old writer and actor with a gold earring and a long blond ponytail. Then he breaks into a rousing chorus of "Happy Birthday."

"Start taking vocal lessons," Buell says.

It's the first day of auditions for the prison theater program, which has been staging plays at Sing Sing for eight years. One of only three such programs in the country, it's drawn support from the local community and Broadway actors and sparked a study by the John Jay College for Criminal Justice, which found that inmate actors have better social skills and fewer conflicts. Most of the actors are in for murders. Most are in for life.

Next up is Kareem, a somber man in a white skullcap. Seventeen years ago, under the name Kelly Watts, he beat a friend to death with his fists after he made a nasty comment to his girlfriend. Buell asks if he's willing to share a role. "I'd be willing to do whatever you want me to do," he says, "including dress in drag."

Next comes Dario Pena, a handsome man with a scar that circumnavigates his head. In a rich and plummy voice he reads a speech from an old English play: "Now in*deed* I am a prisoner! Yes, *now* I feel the *galling* weight of these dis*graceful* chains!"

Buell asks him if he's interested in any particular part.

"I'll play anything—even a dead body."

So Buell has him read for Dead Man Number 1.

The convicts keep coming. Guy Youngblood looks like Kris Kristofferson and reads the roles of Cannibal Pete and Matt Dillon in the same rich pirate burr. Divine Eye has long dreadlocks and massive muscles and sings "Happy Birthday" with showbiz pizzazz, throwing his arms out. Spider is a skinny White guy who looks like a bent altar boy and bows as he exits. Elijah has a Mormon beard and a middle-aged paunch and reads in a British accent straight out of *Masterpiece Theatre*. Patrick has a goatee and a gold tooth and lots of energy and reads for Gravedigger as if he can't wait to bury the whole world. He sings "Happy Birthday" twice.

Then there's Pow Wow. Tall and reserved, he listens with a wary look as Buell says he wrote a part for him, the only role he wrote with a specific person in mind. The scene is about a gladiator who wants to give up fighting and become gentle and kind, but the world won't let him. As he reads it, Pow Wow's eyes go big. "That's exactly how it happened! Did someone tell you? I got into an incident."

"Tell me," Buell demands.

Pow Wow says he was in the yard when someone pushed him into a corner. He had to fight back. He had no choice.

Buell looks pained. "You gotta be like the Virgin Mary for the rest of the show."

"I'm trying."

"No matter what they do, just eat it."

"I do."

Pow Wow shows off a dance move.

"You want me to sing?"

Watching killers sing and dance is an odd thing. First it hits you—gosh, they're nervous and excited, giggly and shy, desperate for appreciation and recognition just like everyone else. Then you think of what they did to get here and you feel ashamed, as if your recognition of their humanity was actually a moment of weakness. *Shouldn't these guys be punished?*

"We're not in the punishment business," says the Sing Sing superintendent, Brian Fischer. "Going to prison is the punishment. Our mandate is a safe, clean facility."

From a pragmatic point of view, he says, inmates who are involved in activities tend to stay out of trouble. They learn to work hard, to commit to something, to defer gratification. Underpaid guards who resent the fully equipped convict weight rooms quickly learn that the inmates with the biggest muscles tend to be the ones who cause the fewest problems. And with convicts going home at an alarming rate—630,000 a year—every bit of self-discipline they pick up is a plus for you and me, their future neighbors.

Fischer doesn't mention the ancient idea that literature and art are an essential part of a person's moral education, deepening our empathy for other people, but that's implicit in the program. Rehabilitation Through the Arts, it calls itself.

But is it true? Can art really rehabilitate a man? Does singing and dancing really heal? Can slapstick save your soul?

By the second week, Pow Wow is out of the show; because of his "incident" and the death threats that followed, he got moved to involuntary protective custody. Eric comes in to audition for his part. A big, handsome guy with a shy way of reading, he laughs when he gets to cuss words. "Can you look real menacing?" Buell asks.

Eric nods, looking utterly harmless.

Afterward, Buell reads out the casting assignments. Youngblood gets Cannibal Pete and Matt Dillon, Rasheed gets Gravedigger, Spider gets Chester and Scurvy Legs, Patrick gets Merry Man Number 1 and . . .

Patrick looks alarmed. "Maid Marian?"

"Not Maid Marian-Merry Man."

In another room, the inmates on the theater steering committee talk about how to fill the holes in the cast. They interviewed three new people on Saturday. Maybe Eric could take on another role.

"He has some trouble reading," Buell points out.

"We'll help him," says Divine Eye.

"That's what we do," Dap says with pride.

At the third session, they have their first read through. It's a dismal, cold day in February and you can barely see the sky through the heavy wire and ancient dirt on the windows. This is the "schoolhouse," a brick building in the middle of the prison grounds. There are blackboards and inspirational posters. The prisoners gather the desks in a circle, each man holding a script in his lap. Most have marked their dialogue with yellow highlighter.

Written by Buell, the play, *Breakin' the Mummy's Code*, is about six convicts who each write separate plays and then splice them together into one ridiculous romp. Buell's main creative goal was lots of parts and lots of costumes, so the play has pirates and gladiators and cowboys and a spy in a tuxedo and even Prince Hamlet of Denmark. It also has lots of play-within-a-play dialogue about prisoners on the stage. "We do these plays for RTA," writes Buell. "And, man, for that little while, there's no walls. We're free. We're soaring."

They act hard. Kareem's reading glasses slide down his nose. Everyone laughs when Rasheed does his cockney accent. When Spider stumbles over the word *misogynist*, four men shout out the correct pronunciation. When Divine Eye starts a full-bore performance of Hamlet's "To be or not to be," it seems almost like a *Saturday Night Live* routine at first, this high-flown language in the mouth of a muscle-bound convict. But he's so serious and passionate that the moment is transformed. *That's* why the groundlings came to see Shakespeare, you realize, not for the sword fights and bear baiting; the heightened language heightened them.

The loudspeaker crackles time.

As the weeks go on, the personalities of the prisoners start to emerge. Youngblood is eager to be known, confessing to a secret marriage and bringing in a sheaf of his poetry. Dap's Mr. Cool, always smiling and collected, locking his line readings early and doing them exactly the same every single time. Winter smolders with granite silence, then flashes a winning smile. Spider is the king of jokes and sheepish grins. Bilal is the diplomat, the organizer, the stage manager. "We have to nip breaks in the bud," he says. "Bathroom is an exception, prayers are an exception, but watch the coffee and tea runs. Otherwise it's not fair to the team. It's imperative we take this seriously."

Gradually their stories come out, too. Dap's real name is David James. He grew up in Queens with an abusive stepfather and a mother so deeply stressed that the tension came out in big red shingles on her skin. He did well in school but chose the life of a rock star, which he got through selling drugs. His luck ran out at twenty-one, eight years ago. Guy Youngblood grew up in Connecticut with his mom, a secretary, tangled with his stepfather, and got into drugs and ended up a teenage runaway living on the street. When he was twenty-five, eighteen years ago, he killed a man in a drug deal. Winter is Lamont Bryant of the Bronx, arrested "due to circumstance rather than criminal talent—a love triangle." He was twenty-five then, six years ago. Spider grew up in a small town near the Canadian border under the name Brian LaBrosse, adopted son of a nurse and a heavy-equipment operator. A high school dropout with a record of minor crimes, he got arrested five years ago for a killing he describes as a hunting accident. Bilal was Dexter Robinson of Brooklyn, stepson of a military officer. He's been inside for twelve years for a double homicide with gang involvement. "If people needed to sleep," he says, "I made them sleep."

With the most shocking story, Kareem turns out to be the most impressive man. Dignified and studious, an elder statesman of the tiers, he's earned a BA and an MA, works as an aide in the family workshop and youth-awareness programs, and teaches a religion class to other inmates. Superintendant Fischer singles him out as a model prisoner worthy of a letter to the parole board, the kind who knows the difference between "making a mistake" and committing a crime.

"I know what resides inside me," Kareem says.

Once, Buell let a homeless man stay at his house for a weekend and the guy ended up staying for two years. After four years of volunteering, it's still emotional for him to go in and out of the prison, walking through all those steel doors and then back out again, free to go to a movie or a store on a whim. He gushes about the prisoners and their breakthroughs and talents.

Time for an acting exercise. Everyone stand in a circle and raise your arms. Get as tall as you can and then get a little taller and then bring your arms down and *feel* tall. That's called taking the stage. "You see actors in real life and they can seem very small," he says, "but onstage they seem very big."

He starts to block scene five. "Have you thought about how funny ancient Egyptians might move?"

With him in charge, giving them permission, silliness slips through the room like a contagious giggle. In the black-plague scene, the convicts mug spectacular deaths, hooting as the bodies pile up on the floor. Buell suggests they come back to life for a second and die again, so they shoot out their legs and gasp for breath and bulge their eyes. "Try to move like you're *rotting*," he says.

Lying on the floor, they squirm and twitch.

Today is a sunny spring day, golden light coming in the venetian blinds. First some stretching exercises and jumping jacks and then the big ending dance number to get everyone pumped. Now meet Kim Breden. She was in *The Phantom of the Opera* in Germany, and she's here to help you sing. "It's all about using the best tools to tell your story," she says. Start with proper breath support and diction. Take a deep belly breath and then hiss it out. "If you have long lines to say, this is a great exercise."

Next she asks them to hum: "Fill your head with sound! Project it to the back of the theater!"

Now smile on the inside. "Listen to what happens to the tone."

"It went up!"

"Yes. Thank you. If you want to bring up the pitch, you can smile inside."

It sounds like a hive of bees, everyone humming, looking for that inner smile.

"Where do you feel it?" she asks.

Elijah points to his nose.

Then they follow her up the scale. "Guys, the vocal cords are a muscle. You must work with them like any other muscle . . . *ma me mi mo mu* . . . "

She takes them up in half steps and nags them about diction: "Every single consonant matters. You are telling a story. You can't leave anything out."

Pretty soon they're booming like marines: "*Hut hut hut. Mutt mutt mutt. Sutt sutt sutt.*"

"Keep that smile inside," she says. "You have to charm the audience."

Waiting for his scene, Winter offers up a rap:

All the time, every time I turn around
I'm falling victim to these temptations.

As a kid, he was curious about the stars and dreamed of becoming an astronomer, he says. But his life seemed to be going in slow motion, and he went from making up rhymes about money and violence to living them. Arrested at seventeen for armed robbery, he spent a year in the Elmira prison. "I thought it was a rite of passage. That's what rappers taught me. That's the bullshit I swallowed."

I'm calling, I'm calling
I'm falling, I'm falling
Walls are closing in,
The doors ain't opening

A couple of years ago, one of the RTA guys heard him rapping in the yard and suggested he give acting a try. He worked with a volunteer named Joanna Chan for five months to develop the character of a fifty-year-old man in August Wilson's *Jitney*. In her sixties, Chan looks and sounds like a sweet Chinese grandma. But she's a political dissident and a Maryknoll nun and a published playwright and a person of infinite persistence, and the prisoners have surprisingly intense feelings for her. "I *love* Joanna Chan," Winter says. "I would do anything for that woman." The more he studied his character, the more he understood him. "It was like putting on my grandfather's clothes," he says.

Many of the prisoners tell similar stories. Kareem was in rehearsals for weeks, playing a man whose life went sour when his son went to jail, when he finally realized he was playing his own father. Seeing it through the character made it easier to face. One day in the visiting room, he said, "I'm sorry for what I put you through. I put you through a lot."

He had never said that to his father before.

Late in April, they start rehearsing in the prison auditorium, a big, echoing space made out of brick and steel. Even though there are no guards in sight, everyone stays serious and focused. "Next scene!" Buell calls. "Where's Zakariedies? Where's Double-O?"

In the audience, Superintendent Fischer sits with two charity-minded women from the local community. The old curtain is torn and frayed, patched by convicts with fishing line, and they're here to decide whether to donate $4,600 for a new one.

Double-O comes out in character, shadowboxing. "We specialize in grotesque violence—line?"

"Skewering! Flailing!"

He picks up the line and keeps going, working into a crazy, smiling-killer thing that is genuinely scary. "Muzzle the gladiator!" Buell cries, happily.

Grinning, Double-O makes it bigger. By the closing dance, he stomps out like a monster and keeps on dancing in the background till the music stops, giddy with the moment.

The women agree to pay for the curtain.

Katherine Vockins is the founder and producer of RTA. A thin and elegant businesswoman from a nearby suburb, she was working in marketing and remembering her teenage theater days when she heard about a group of prisoners who had an interest in playwriting. She went in for a look and came out hooked. Tonight she drags in three big suitcases stuffed with costumes and waits at the gate as a guard checks items off a list: one purple cloak, one wedding veil, one pink full-length gown, one pirate hat, eight cowboy hats, eight eye patches . . .

In the auditorium, saws buzz and the actors lounge in the house seats, waiting. A crew of prisoners has been working for two weeks on the sets. Two carved planks move back and forth for waves, a bathtub doubles as a boat and a bier, a mast with a Jolly Roger suggests a pirate ship, and there's a bike made entirely of wood that says MY SON IS AN HONOR STUDENT AT SING SING VOCATIONAL. Vockins gathers everyone and asks them to be vigilant about costumes and props. In fourteen shows, she says, they've never lost anything. "Be responsible."

"Let the dragon out!" Bilal barks.

It's a chaotic scene. Youngblood arrives late and has to do his speech in prison green. Thai Chi forgets to change a set. Random prisoners drift through the auditorium on their way to somewhere else. There's a new actor filling in for Double-O, who dropped out of the show due to creative differences. Buell yells, "Double time! Exit fast! I'm tired of people walking slow!" Afterward, he tells them to speak louder and more clearly, be aware of where the floor mics are.

But backstage, Youngblood has a dark expression. "My wife was supposed to come, and she didn't show up," he whispers. "I don't know why. And I blew my lines. And I can't dance to music."

In his funk, he starts to vent. He wanted to try out for the lead, but let's face it, the program is geared toward African Americans. They say it's a family, but it's not. "Me and Spider are the only White guys, and we get the most foolish parts."

Buell overhears him. "Leave it behind!" he says. "You can be happy here! Be happy!"

"I'm in a mood," Youngblood says.

Then it's opening night and the prisoners of B block file into the auditorium. They're the roughest guys at Sing Sing, the hardest audience, big guys with huge muscles and scarred faces. Backstage, the cast forms a circle, holding hands. "Now is the time when all the hard work pays off," Buell says.

After a moment of silence, they shout in unison: "*RTA!*"

The show starts slow, with a trickle of laughs for physical humor—a bouncing cannonball, Kareem's shtick with a scarf and a beret, Winter pretending to stab himself. Joke by dumb joke, the audience warms up. They applaud when Maid Marian slugs Robin Thug. A play on Snoop Dogg's "fa shizzle my nizzle" routine goes over big. They love the sawtooth waves and Hamlet's unexpected dignity. In this harsh world of stone and steel, the silliness feels like an achievement, a judo flip that turns pain into hope. Youngblood's wife came to visit this morning and they got into a fight so bad he had to walk out to keep from getting crazy, but he gets a laugh when he lists all the antidepressants he's taking to survive cowboy life. Even the mistakes seem like a metaphor for how to live. When a crew member rushes a forgotten prop out in midscene, Dap just grins and makes it part of the scene: "That wasn't there a minute ago!"

When he dances the waltz, his partner looks so delicate and lovely in her lacy white dress, the house goes quiet. Row after row, the fearsome men of B block light up with gentle smiles.

When it's over, B block gives them a standing ovation. "Thank you!" Kareem shouts out. "We do it for y'all because we love you!" Backstage, the feelings are surprisingly intense, an explosion of sudden joy and brotherhood that's very moving to see. Spider lifts Dap up off the floor and Kareem hugs Bilal hard and Bilal tells everyone, "I'm proud of you, I'm proud of you." Rasheed is thrilled with his first performance. "The *crowd* was supportive," he says, amazed. Divine Eye is beaming. "Did you see how quiet it got when I did the Hamlet joint? 'Oh shit, he's really doing it!'"

In this moment, there seems to be no doubt: Art heals, slapstick saves, killers can become comedians. Even Youngblood is happy. Soon he will go back to brooding on his troubled marriage and wasted life. But right now he wants to bask in the moment. "I got to be someone else for a while," he says.

He grins and tips his cowboy hat.

JFK praised him. David Halberstam scorned him. The CIA consumed him. Rising out of World War II military intelligence operations, John H. Richardson became the consummate cold warrior, one of the elite CIA station chiefs dispatched to the hottest global hot spots. Along with him, he brought a wife and one very un-CIA-like child of the sixties—his only son, the author.

Mom calls. Dad is in the hospital, on oxygen. It's his heart. I fly down. They live in Mexico in a big adobe house with cool tile floors and high ceilings. Servants move quietly through the rooms. Mom greets me at the door, telling me through tears that she found him last night flopped across the bed with his legs hanging off the edge. He couldn't lift his feet onto the bed, so he just lay there like flotsam for an hour before he started calling for help. When she finally woke up, he apologized for bothering her. Then I laugh, and she smiles through her tears, because it's just so Dad. He's always so polite, so maddeningly self-denying. Sometimes my mom cries out: "Don't ask me what I want! Just tell me what you want!"

I go into his room, and his face is puffy and red, and he looks so very weak. With his dentures out and his head back, he looks like cartoon of an old codger, lips sucked back over his gums and grizzled chin jutting out. One yellowed tooth stands out in the black hole of his mouth. He's like an apple that's been sitting on a shelf for months, all dried out and sucked down into itself. But when he sees me standing there, his face brightens. He's so grateful to see me, so relieved—and he immediately starts worrying that I've abandoned my important professional responsibilities to come.

A few minutes later, he gets up to go to the bathroom. I've seen him hobbling around the house for years now and I'm used to frail—he's been juggling congestive heart failure, osteoporosis, cirrhosis, and about a half dozen other major illnesses for almost a decade. But now, the nurse takes one arm, and I take the other, and he leans over so far he's actually hanging by his arms, chest nearly parallel to the floor. He goes three steps and pauses, rests against the bureau, then takes five more steps and rests again. Glancing sideways, I see gray in his cheeks, a whitish gray like dirty marble.

He makes us wait outside the bathroom. He won't be helped in there. So we stand right outside the door, and when the toilet flushes I peek in and see him shuffle to the sink. He's wearing blue pajamas with a tissue folded into the breast pocket like a pocket square. He leans down with his elbows hard against the yellow tiles and washes his hands. On his way out, he stops to put the toilet seat down.

My father was a spy, a high-ranking member of the CIA, one of those idealistic men who came out of World War II determined to save the world from tyranny. Like so many of his colleagues, he ended up bitter at a world that mocked and frustrated and finally vilified him. His bitterness was the mystery of my childhood, turning me stubborn and defiant. Like most sons of unhappy fathers, I had a hole inside me cut to the shape of his sadness, a hole I tried to fill in all the usual ways and never did, because happiness would be too much of a betrayal. My miseries were a tribute to his own—a fucked-up gesture of fucked-up solidarity. So I was always leaving home and coming back and leaving again and coming back again, and often on these visits I would interview him, trying to bridge the gulf between us in the only way I knew. But whenever I pulled out my tape recorder, he would remind me that he had taken an oath of silence. That was always the first thing he said: "You know, son, I took an oath of silence."

In bed at night, he's wheezing and gasping so hard I think he's going to die with each breath. But he goes on as always, worrying about Mom and whether she's adequately covered by insurance and his pension, ground we've been over a million times before. He gives me advice on renting the house our after he dies. He philosophizes for my benefit, as he has all his long life.

"Accidents play such a large part in our lives," he says. "I don't mean accident like car accidents. If it hadn't been for the war, I would have had a very different life."

I've heard this a million times before.

Then he asks me if the doctor thinks this "slump" will get better. In my family we tell the truth, always have, sometimes more than we should, so I say I don't think it will. "There's always a chance, but I don't think so."

He seems relieved at that, seems to relax. Behind his breath, there's a rattle deep in his throat or deeper.

This life began eighty-four years ago in Burma. His father was a wildcat oil engineer from Louisiana (a proud man's way of saying he learned his trade on the job), and his mother was a tough Texas farm girl named Annie Strelsky—Dad never knew if she was Jewish or Polish or Russian and always told me it didn't matter because we were Americans. After the Burma oil boom ended, they moved to Whittier, California, a Quaker town surrounded by orange and lemon groves. Richard Nixon was one class ahead of my dad all through high school and college. Although Dad's parents seem to have been freethinkers—his father was a Freemason and fumed around the house about the night riders who attacked Blacks moving into the area—Dad became pious at a young age, teaching Sunday school at a Baptist church. He studied Greek and Latin and by high school graduation could read Cicero in the original. At fourteen, he saw his father die, and he would remember until the day of his own death the sound of his father's last cry and the sight of his body giving one last jerk on the bed. Around that time, he discovered Will Durant's books on philosophy and plunged into study so deeply that within a few years, he suffered some kind of library-induced nervous breakdown and lost his faith in God.

So he transferred from Whittier to Berkeley and the Romantic poets—his letters home mention Pater, Shelley, Keats, Byron, Wordsworth, and Swinburne. He began wearing a "flowing, multicolored tie." He tried to join the Communist Party, but they wouldn't have him. He swore to live the life of the mind at whatever cost. "Most of us are satisfied with too little," he wrote a friend, "and we never live even though we think that we do. We're pygmies, we're all the hateful, disgusting things that Swift said that we were, and the damnable thing about it all is that we seem complacently, oily content about the whole matter. By the Lord I'll escape this pygmy state if I have to spend the rest of my life doing it!"

After finishing his degree, he went to Paris, where he studied at the Sorbonne and earned pocket money by cataloging the pornography library of a wealthy French homosexual. After a year of that, he bicycled around Ireland and moved to Germany to study at the University of Heidelberg, where he lived in a *kameradschaft* house with a group of athletic young men who tried to pump him with the glories of national socialism. From his letters home, I get the impression that he was attracted by their health and vigor, but then he saw Hitler speak and was so disturbed, he went back home to study sociology. As he told me years later, he felt that literature hadn't given him "the vocabulary" to argue with those vigorous young Germans. But then his younger brother died of a self-inflicted gunshot wound that was or was not suicide—Dad always believed it was—and Dad drifted through a teaching certificate and a year as an English teacher before moving to the University of Chicago to work on a PhD in anthropology. When the Japanese attacked Pearl Harbor, he tried to sign up right away, but his glasses got him listed 4F. In 1943, his mother died of cancer in his arms and the Army noticed he spoke French and German and asked if he'd mind "wandering the battlefields at night taking papers off of corpses"—which is when he began the long transformation from that romantic young boy in the flowing tie to the complicated and difficult and decent and cruel and tender man I knew as my father.

This afternoon, Dad's pulse goes down to 50 (from 80), and he gasps down lungfuls of air with his head back and lips wide apart, like someone getting mouth-to-mouth. He starts complaining about pain in his chest and pain in his right arm, and then his face seems to slacken into a death mask, his lower lip retracting over his gums almost to the back of his tongue. The nurse shows me the pulse on the chart and goes to call the doctor. Then my sister and the nurse and I all sit around him, stroking him—something we learned from the nurse, a squat young woman whose inward calm is very soothing to us all. At first, I felt awkward about it, stroking his arm for a long time before I got up the nerve to take his hand. I can tell my sister, Jennifer, feels awkward about touching him, too. We are the kind of family that never touched until we said goodbye and then gave each other a hard and awkward hug.

Later, when Jennifer leaves and we are alone in the room, he apologizes. "I'm sorry this is taking so long."

We did not get along when I was a kid. He was distant and preoccupied, and I was (I am told) a natural-born smart-ass. By the time I turned fourteen, I was sneaking out to take drugs, shoplift, and commit acts of petty vandalism, which on at least one occasion prompted the intervention of the local constabulary. That was also the summer he told me he worked for the CIA, but I can't claim high political motives for my rebellion. The only possible connection is that in 1968 he was the kind of guy who would work for the CIA and I was the kind of guy who wanted to drop acid and listen to the White Album over and over. That summer, we moved to Korea, where he brooded on the world's most rigid totalitarian state (just twenty-six miles north of our house!) and I dated Korean bar girls and smoked bushels of dope. Military intelligence officers wrote reports on my activities and sent them to my father, who gave me lectures on being a "representative of my country." Which seemed rather comical to me, since all my fellow representatives were just as whacked as I was; my friend Adrienne had a habit of carving her arm with a razor, Karen was dabbling in heroin, and Peter dropped out of high school and into a reefer haze. So I would bait my father at dinner by defending communism—all your better hippies live on communes, don't they? He would get insanely angry, sputtering his way into a lecture on totalitarianism before leaving the table in disgust. Once I called him paranoid and he exploded into the most gratifyingly paranoid rage I have ever seen. It all came to a boil the day I got beat up by an MP—he called me a girl; I gave him the finger—who charged me with the crime he had committed, assault. When Dad came to get me with his chauffeur and his big black car, he took me to the office of the army general in charge of all Korea and made me apologize for forcing that poor MP to beat me with his club. Not long after that, those helpful men at military intelligence sent Dad a note saying I was a "known user of LSD," and then the army psychiatrists had a crack at me, and before long I was on a plane back to the States—sixteen years old and on my own. If I couldn't get into a college early, I was going to have to support myself. Thanks a lot, Dad. And fuck you very much.

The nurse keeps examining Dad's fingertips, which are turning blue. This is a bad sign. She takes his pulse and goes to call the doctor. Meanwhile, Dad keeps asking the time, which seems ominously significant. Then he keeps trying to tell us something, and Jennifer and I sit close on the edge of the bed, convinced that these are his last words. "*Gee fi ohf*," he says. "*Gee fof*."

Finally, I figure it out. He's trying to say G505—the satellite setting for the *Evans and Novak* show.

"We're here with you," I say.

He smiles sweetly.

In Italy, Dad spent his time rounding up spies with his two best friends, Gordon Messing ("the sloppiest soldier in the US armed forces") and Gordon Mason ("handsome, debonair, witty, sardonic, a great lover"). He also fell in love for the first time, with an Italian baroness whose husband was a fascist officer. And managed to stop an antifascist riot in a small mountain town by climbing onto the hood of his jeep and lecturing the mob on "Aristotle's iron law of politics, to the effect that the anarchy and lawlessness of violence leads to tyranny." But by the end of the war, his romanticism had burned off completely. A letter he wrote to a high school friend shows him changed right down to the rhythms of his prose: "I feel older than the three years would have normally caused, sadder and very tired. I drank hard, played poker and shot craps, made love indiscriminately like all soldiers do. In three years I have hardly read a book, and feel now almost too restless to spend a single evening at home."

Transferred to Salzburg, Dad began arresting Nazis at the rate of fifty a month. (Later, the Austrian Ministry of the Interior officially declared his county "the best and most thoroughly de-Nazified country in all of Austria.") After each conviction, he sat his prisoner down in his office and handed him a scrapbook he had compiled of magazine photos of the camps at Auschwitz and Buchenwald. "I had come to hate the Nazi system," he wrote me years later, "and I mean hate it emotionally as well as intellectually. You will remember that when you were a boy I took you to the Jefferson Memorial in Washington and asked you to remember the words he wrote, carved out above his statue: 'I have sworn upon the altar of God eternal hostility against every form of tyranny over the mind of man.' No better sentence has been written in the English language."

One day, a Soviet official came to Dad's office to bluster against America's recent refusal to repatriate White Russians to Soviet camps, shouting at Dad in "a bullying, overbearing manner, typical of the Soviet style." When Dad lost his patience and threatened to have the MPs drag him away, the official's attitude immediately changed to wheedling conciliation. That made a big impression. "All subsequent experience has convinced me that you can deal with the Communists and the Nazis of this world—and all bullyboy types—only from a position of strength. Their basic human philosophy, if you can call it human, is that of the bully—despise and abuse weakness, defer to strength."

Dad never stops giving me instructions. The doctor told him that fruit is good for you and he wants me to know, too. "Remember that, son—fruit is good for you." He gets obsessed with a lost pill; it was in his bedclothes, he keeps saying. Did he drop it? Did he forget to take it? Should he take another one? A minute later, he worries if the nurse has taken a lunch break. I send her off and help him to the bathroom, and when I hear the flush, I open the door a crack and see him leaning over to wipe off the edge of the toilet bowl. He apologizes for taking so long.

From Salzburg, Dad went to Vienna. Those were the *Third Man* years, when Vienna was a free-for-all of spies, smugglers, and escaping Russian royalists. The Soviets were rushing into the vacuum left by the Nazis, and their tactics were so brutal that despite the size of Dad's operation—two hundred agents covering half of Eastern Europe—spying on them proved bitterly difficult. Austrian agents often disappeared to firing squads or prison camps. One was stabbed and thrown off a train. Ever the scholar, Dad began reading anticommunist writers like George Orwell and Arthur Koestler. He bought complete sets of the works of Lenin and Marx (still in our library to this day). Years later, one of his colleagues told me that some CIA agents just wanted adventure, travel, notches on the belt. Not Dad. "Your father *believed*," he said, with a lot of respect and maybe a bit of sadness.

As the forties came to a close, the revolution in China and the rumblings of war in Korea seemed to threaten fresh conflict, possibly even another world war. In 1950, a Soviet-inspired coup attempt in Austria sparked riots in several cities. In Vienna, the police almost lost control, and my mother and father—they had met and quickly married that year—were nearly trapped behind the Soviet lines. The atmosphere became so dangerous that Dad's bodyguard stayed at their home every night, sleeping at the foot of the stairs.

Dad wants to hear about the news. I tell him that yesterday they made peace in Ireland.

He's puzzled. "You're in denial?"

"No, Dad, peace in Ireland."

He still loves talking foreign policy, and when I read him the news summary from *Slate* magazine, he says he likes Netanyahu and feels the Israelis can't ever tolerate a Palestinian state.

"Do you think you could eat some Jell-O?" I ask.

He frowns again. "Time to go?"

Then to Athens, in those years one of the biggest CIA posts in the world. Dad and his agents ran operations against the Soviets from Kazakhstan to Hungary, including difficult targets like Bulgaria and

Romania. They broadcast free-world news in fourteen languages, dropped leaflets ll over Eastern Europe, maintained their own airport and air force of a half-dozen planes and a few boats, too. Agent after agent disappeared into Albania, never to return. But Dad never told me about all this. It was Gordon Mason, Dad's old friend and chief of external operations of the Athens station, who finally filled me in. My complaints about the old man's stubborn reticence brought only a smile. "The chief of station in many ways outranks the ambassador in power—the number of people, the prestige, the money, the assets, the contacts," he told me. "Your father was involved in a lot of powerful dealings with a lot of powerful people in the world. But he never flaunted it. He was very modest. You look at him now, and you wonder at the power this man held in his lifetime."

He's too weak to wash his hands. I can tell it upsets him, so I wipe them with a wet washcloth and dry them with a towel. When we get back to the bed, I try to get him to sit up, which is better for his lungs, but he shakes his head. "Why do the so-called right things, when they'll just prolong this condition?"

He lies back, eyes closed, talking intermittently. Some of it is hard to follow. At one point, he says in a tone of surprise, "It's Jimmy Hoffa!"

I tease him. "So you're finally giving up the secrets!"

His eyes open, and he asks what I said. I repeat the whole exchange a couple of times until he understands. Then he gets somber. "It has always been off-limits for the agency to conduct domestic operations," he says.

Dad was ordered to Vietnam early in 1962. When he arrived, the war seemed to be going pretty well, and he plunged into work on the "strategic hamlet" program, a controversial series of armed settlements intended to slow the Vietcong infiltration. Four years in the Philippines had made him one of the CIA's most seasoned counterinsurgency specialists. He met weekly with Ngo Dinh Nhu, President Ngo Dinh Diem's intensely controversial brother. (Nhu later orchestrated the attacks on the rebellious Buddhists.) But toward the end of the year, the Vietcong began to win significant battles, and the Buddhist uprising began, at which point the American reporters on the scene began painting Diem as a paranoid autocrat who didn't have enough popular support to win the war—just another American puppet gone bad. The portrait was a gross simplification but had a pivotal effect on American policy: President Kennedy reacted by sending in a new ambassador, who treated Diem with undisguised contempt. That was Henry Cabot Lodge, still a controversial figure in my house—my mother loathes him. By the summer of 1963, Dad was a lonely figure in the Saigon embassy, the only ranking official who still supported Diem. As he often told me later, he admired Diem's courage and honesty and saw no "credible alternative" among the squabbling generals who would be king. By the time of Nhu's raids on the Buddhist pagodas, Dad was so linked to the Diem regime that he was suspected of complicity in the attacks. "That morning Richardson was a tired and shaken man," David Halberstam wrote in his first Vietnam book, *The Making of a Quagmire*. "He refuted the rumor immediately. 'It's not true,' he said. 'We just didn't know. We just didn't *know*, I can assure you.'"

Then Dad received a fateful cable from his superiors at the CIA. On orders from "the highest authority"—which Dad took to mean President Kennedy—he was instructed that unless he had "overwhelming objections," he was to support Ambassador Lodge and take the actions necessary to mount a coup. Reluctantly, Dad obeyed, sending the legendary CIA agent Lucien Connie (always "Lou" at my house) to encourage General Duong Van "Big" Minh, the primary coup plotter. On August 28, Dad sent a cable to CIA headquarters that later appeared in the Pentagon Papers, a cable he would come to regret: SITUATION HERE HAS REACHED POINT OF NO RETURN . . . WE ALL UNDERSTAND THAT THE EFFORT MUST SUCCEED AND THAT WHATEVER NEEDS TO BE DONE ON OUR PART MUST BE DONE.

The coup fizzled, and the *Times of Vietnam* ran a front-page story accusing Dad of trying to overthrow the government, which got him a place on the hotly rumored assassination lists. Meanwhile, someone began a behind-the-scenes campaign to get Dad fired. On October 2, the *Washington Daily News* ran a story by a Scripps Howard correspondent named Richard Starnes that accused Dad twice by name of disobeying direct orders from Lodge. The headline was "ARROGANT" CIA DISOBEYING ORDERS IN SO. VIET NAM. Citing a "very high United States source," Starnes called Dad's career in Vietnam "a dismal chronicle of bureaucratic arrogance, obstinate disregard of orders, and unrestrained thirst for power." Two days later, Halberstam corrected Starnes on the front page of the *New York Times*, writing that there was "no evidence that the CIA chief has directly countermanded any orders by the ambassador," but he also used Dad's name. "Outed" as a CIA agent, Dad was finished. A day later, he flew back to Washington, where the CIA hid him away for two weeks while newspapers all over the world ran stories about his ouster. The Washington *Evening Star* ran one of the few sympathetic takes: "The crime Mr. Richardson is said to have committed is truly fascinating. He is being charged in the bars of Saigon with declining to overthrow the government of South Viet Nam—incredibobble, as Pogo would say."

One month later, Diem and Nhu were deposed and shot to death, leaving my father with plenty of time to brood on the caveat the CIA chiefs had slipped into that fatal cable: "unless you have overwhelming objections." In retrospect, it seems to have been put there just to give him something to torture himself with for the rest of his life.

Tonight I'm testing Dad's new painkillers. There's mariachi music next door, the jacarandas are in bloom, and Dad's blood pressure just plunged from 100 over 60 to 80 over 50. He sees Jennifer in the hall and doesn't seem to recognize her. "There's the lady who is going to give me my Metamucil," he says. But he still puts on his slippers every time he goes to the bathroom, and he still insists on having a napkin folded into the pocket of his pajamas.

Lying back on the bed with his eyes closed, he asks me: "When did this happen and how? This condition?"

I don't know what to say.

He turns to my mother: "I'm sorry to be such a problem."

"You're not a problem to me," she answers.

"That's important," he says.

I was nine and ten in Vietnam. I remember a French school with chickens in the yard, and Buddhist monks exorcising our house, and the morning I sneaked past the guards at the gate of our house to go to the marketplace. I remember chasing a girl around a schoolyard, trying to untie the ribbon of her dress. I don't remember the day my sister was watching a Disney movie in a local theater and bombs exploded in the lobby, or the day our nanny foiled a kidnapping attempt by hitting a cabdriver with her umbrella and hustling my sister and me out of the cab, or the day one of the kids at my school tried to imitate the Buddhist suicides by pouring gasoline on himself and lighting a match. But I do remember the day my dad didn't come home and my mom sat around without turning on the lights and I got shushed by the servants. Years later, I learned that his helicopter had been shot down in the jungle and she thought he was dead.

Dad tells me that he's been hearing music—emotional music, orchestral, like a movie score. But there is no music playing. A day later, he says he's figured out where the music is coming from. "This music—it's produced by us," he says. "It's a subsidiary of ours."

Later, he murmurs: "Yeah, this is the tail end." He looks at me. "I hope this never happens to you—to be partly killed."

Later still, he frowns, puzzled: "This seems to be just a fragment of me," he says.

Most of Dad's stories are self-deprecating. Talking about Vienna, he tells me not about how powerful he was but about mistakes he made. One time, he was crossing through the Soviet zone and absentmindedly left maps on the backseat detailing the location of military forces in Yugoslavia. Along the way, he gave a young Pole a ride, and when they got to the checkpoint, the Russians became very suspicious and arrested the Pole. "They didn't touch the maps, which would have shown me to be a goddamned spy," Dad told me once, giving me his look of mock alarm. "If they had looked at the maps, I might not be here talking to you."

Years later, an officer of Dad's named Bill Hood centered a spy novel called *Mole* on the Vienna station. Dad appears as the savvy, tough spymaster Joel Roberts. "After six years in Austria," Hood wrote, "Roberts knew every alley in Vienna's *Innere Stadt*." The book tells the true story of the first Soviet counterspy ever recruited by the US, but Dad's version of the story is pretty undramatic. "As I recall, he approached some American at his car, got in, and defected," Dad told me. "Later, he was uncovered by the Soviet service and I think executed."

But what about convincing him to go back? Wasn't that a big feather in your cloak?

"I suppose it was, but it was very accidental," he said. "I don't think we deserved any particular merit."

The next day, my sister comes running into the kitchen. Dad's in a lot of pain, wants a shot of something, wants us to take him to the hospital. "I think this is it," she says. But when I get the doctor on the phone, he tells me that once we go to a hospital they'll hook Dad up to machines and keep him alive as long as they can, no matter how vegetative he might get. None of us want that. We stall, and the crisis passes. Dad lies back with his eyes closed, talking out of dreams: "The CIA contact . . ."

I can't catch the rest.

After Vietnam, Dad got kicked upstairs to a desk job as director of training. He brooded and drank, had a heart attack, argued with his superiors about training methods. His friend Frank Wisner (a legendary CIA agent who played an unfortunate role in the Bay of Pigs fiasco) had a mental breakdown and committed suicide. And the war started going to hell, and the hippies started protesting, and, looking back on it now, I can see how it must have seemed bizarre to them, these idealistic men who were just trying to save the world. Suddenly, the very people they had sworn to protect despised them! Nobody cared that most of those CIA excesses were done under orders from American presidents, that it was really the sainted John F. Kennedy who spilled the blood that splashed on Dad. It didn't fit into the sixties script: The hard old men were the bad guys, and, by repudiating them, America would somehow become innocent again.

One day, Dad got a letter from a Vietnamese colonel named Le Quang Tung, who had been the head of Nhu's notorious Special Forces troops, the ones that raided the Buddhist temples. Tung said he was facing a firing squad and wanted to apologize; he was sorry for believing the rumors about Dad and now knew that Dad had never wanted to support the coup.

Dad threw away the letter. A few years ago, I harassed him about it. Didn't he care about history?

He gave me a pitying smile. "I have a feeling history is a pretty vain thing," he said.

We watch sitcoms in the study, then talk. Dad's voice has become a whispery tissue. "I remember the old days in Vienna," he says. "Dean was the youngest major in the Army."

Dean is my uncle, another spy. He's an ocean away, also dying of cancer.

Then we watch *Spin City*, and Dad smiles all the way through it. When it's over, the nurse helps him to bed. "It was a good night," he says.

A few years ago, I had lunch in Georgetown with a couple of Dad's old CIA cronies, Bronson Tweedy and Dave Whipple. Both were age-spotted and bald, with a kind of merry irony. They remembered Dad as a compulsive coffee drinker who had "a slightly ponderous way of expressing himself," as a "tough guy" who took controversial stands. They said he was one of the best, a "pillar" of the clandestine services. They even remembered certain improbable nights in Vienna when he danced to gypsy music till dawn. Then I asked them if they knew why he was so depressed and bitter after Vietnam. At first, they talked about his clashes with the CIA hierarchy and his impolitic but apparently unyielding conviction that the best field agents should be rotated into teaching jobs (first I'd heard of that). Then Tweedy sighed. "One of the reasons was he knew he was serving in a losing war."

Whipple nodded slowly. "An awful lot of people were depressed then."

At ten this morning, Dad wakes out of a nap and calls for me. As I help him into the study, my sister goes to get herself breakfast, but Dad waves his hand. "I think she should be in on this," he says. Dad sits on his little Greek chair waiting. He's hooked up to an oxygen tank, breathing through thin plastic tubes. Every few minutes, he spits blood into a kidney-shaped dish, dabbing at his lips with a napkin.

Finally we're all ready, and he begins. "I feel we're not making any progress," he says. "I feel . . . I feel"— he jabs a finger at his chest—"that this could just go on and on. So I want you to call Mike and talk to him."

Mike is his doctor. What Dad means is that he wants me to talk to Mike about giving him some kind of suicide shot. Dad pauses to spit into the dish, and I carry it to the bathroom and wash it out, trying not to look at the bloody phlegm.

"I suppose I could go off the machine," he says, meaning the oxygen. I look over at my mother. As it happens, this very morning a friend of hers sent over some morphine left over from the death of her own husband. I tell Dad about this and say we could always put a batch of it by his bedside if he wants. When he frowns, I try to reassure him, because I know exactly what he's thinking. "It's not like your brother," I say.

"I've always felt bad about my brother's suicide," he says. "I wouldn't want the grandchildren to think their grandfather did that."

"You put up a great fight for eighty-four years, Dad," I say. "It's not like you're taking the easy way out."

My mother and my sister are weeping. The maid vacuums in the hallway.

"I know you feel like it's dragging on," I continue, "but the doctors say it'll just be a week or two more. You're not in pain, your brain is still sharp—and Clinton still hasn't been booted out of office. Why not let nature take its course?"

He seems pleased by that. "Just a week or two?" he says.

I nod.

"And if you start to suffer or just feel you have reached the end of your rope, then know that we do have this alternative," I say. "Talk to me. You don't have to tell Jennifer or Mom. Just come to me."

"Okay, then, we'll wait one more week."

Then we talk about dosage and doctors and make a few terrible jokes about Christianity while my mother and my sister weep nonstop.

"Well that's it, then," Dad finally says. "I think we've covered it all."

But I want to add something. "Dad, I just want to say, I admire you for looking at this straight in the eyes."

He seems very pleased by that. "All right then," he says, with a bit of the old authority. "Go on to what you were doing."

The early years of retirement were the bad years, when Dad earned his cirrhosis bruises. When the dark mood took him, he'd fasten on his completely imaginary money problems or some social error—he was obsessed with politeness to strangers—and pick at it until we were all bloody.

On one binge, he started talking about the Diem coup. He told me that obeying Kennedy's order was the biggest regret of his life. So drunk by then that he may have even cried a little, he said that he wished he had resigned instead of obeying that order. But it came from the president of the United States of America, dammit, with that terrible caveat.

Digging around in my mother's desk a few years ago, I found a series of cryptic notes in my father's handwriting. "Framework of guerrilla war," they began. "Operational involvement vs. analytic detachment. Colby & light at the end of the tunnel. Abandonment of Meos—80,000—one of keenest pangs of defeat—fare of those allied with us. Nat'l interest—cold blooded. Cut our losses but written in human blood."

At the end of these notes, under the heading "Worst episode of my CIA service," I found this:

Why didn't I protest more?

Machine gunner image—carrying out orders mentality

Highest authority and centralized information and judgement

Excessive modesty

Pension?

Conclusion—lack of sufficient conviction in thesis that Diem was dispensable.

After finding these notes, I asked my father what they meant. "I was probably thinking about that cable that said, Unless you have *overriding objections* to the decision of the president, you should carry out the coup plans," he told me.

And the line about excessive modesty?

"I don't have any comment on that."

Pension?

"That was probably a crude self-interest consideration," he said. "I suppose self-interest plays a role in most people's decisions."

I told him I doubted it played a role in his.

"Have it your way," he said.

Late that night, about two, Dad wanders into the study where I am sleeping and asks, "What do you call those pills?"

"Morphine," I say.

Once, about a year ago, I reminded him that President Kennedy praised him on his fiftieth birthday.

"Kennedy praised me on my birthday?"

I had the quote right there and read it to him. "I know that the transfer of Mr. John Richardson, who is a very dedicated public servant, has led to surmises, but I can just assure you flatly that the CIA has not carried out independent activities but has operated under close control of the Director of Central Intelligence, operating with the cooperation of the National Security Council and under my instructions."

Dad frowned. "I don't remember Kennedy praising me," he said.
"It was on the front page of the *New York Times*," I told him.
He shook his head and shrugged. "I don't remember."

Dad hasn't eaten for three days. The guy who runs the nursing service suggests a synthetic-morphine drip (Mexico forbids real morphine out of deference to the US drug obsession), so I get Dad's doctor on the phone, and he agrees to write the prescription for this packet that Dad can carry around with him like a cassette recorder. They stick a needle into his belly to start the drip. An hour later, Dad goes into the bathroom and tries to rip it out. I try to convince him to leave it in, and he stands there, his pants around his ankles, saying he just doesn't like it and doesn't want to be hooked up to anything and just doesn't like it, dammit. My mother reminds him how he hated the oxygen mask at first and how he fought the catheter when he needed that last year, and finally he gives in and sits watching *Crossfire*. But as the day goes on, he gets more befuddled and scared. I hate what this is doing to his dignity.

I get angry at the bullshit media cartoons of cold-blooded CIA agents. I'm still annoyed with Don DeLillo because he told an interviewer that the real CIA wasn't as interesting to him as the idea of the CIA as one of the "churches that hold the final secrets," like it's all just a metaphor for the amusement of pretentious novelists. Other countries don't do this. We don't do it with Army Intelligence or the NSA or the FBI. But onto the CIA, we project all our anxieties about being grown-ups in an ugly world. And it's so easy to point the finger. So easy to sit in an office and write critiques. What's not easy is to choose between the possibility of a global gulag and the lives of thousands of innocent Vietnamese or Guatemalans or Nicaraguans and then to live with that choice—alone, as my father did. And on pile the critics with political motives of their own, which makes them just as dirty as the people who actually take action without the accompanying tragic knowledge, so they gas on and on about poor Salvador Allende because they like those Chilean folksingers, dammit, but Diem—well, hell, wasn't he a bad guy? Didn't he deserve to die? And if I seem a little intemperate about it right now, it's because the *New York Times* fought this gutless paper war right down to my father's obituary, finding some asshole journalist who would say that Dad was sort of a good guy after all because he changed his mind about Vietnam—changed it to agree with the *New York Times!*—even though I told the fucking obit writer over and over that I didn't think he ever really changed his mind, except briefly in a moment of great pressure that he spent the rest of his life regretting. Fucking assholes.

He sits in the study with the oxygen tube wrapped from nose to tonsure like Salvador Dali's mustache, and he raises three fingers. "What is that?" he asks.

"It's the morphine, Dad," I say.

This is our new secret code.

Then he starts joking around about turning his back on our cat, which has a vicious streak, giving us that goofy old look of mock alarm—a face I now make to my own kids. "You've still got your sense of humor," I say.

He smiles. "Two things, son," he says. "The first is humor, and the second is courage. I'd like you to tell the grandchildren."

He smiles at the nurse, his face in profile so thin and noble. I want to draw him, to take a photo, to keep this moment somehow. Then Mom comes in and leans down for a kiss. "Long voyage," he says, smiling at her with those bright beady death eyes.

When I was reading up on the old man, I came across a cable written by David Halberstam to his editors at the *New York Times*, dismissing the work of a reporter who'd written articles defending the Diem government. SHE SPENT MOST OF HER TIME INTERVIEWING HEAD OF CIA BRACKET NOW THOROUGHLY DISCREDITED UNBRACKET . . .

In bed a few hours later, I couldn't sleep. Thoroughly discredited? What an arrogant jerk Halberstam was! The fucking guy was sneering at my dad two days after he landed in Saigon! I'm not making this up. It's in his book—two days off the plane, and he thought he knew more about Vietnam than the head of the fucking CIA!

Until that moment, I didn't realize how much I wanted Dad to be right—about Diem, about communism, about everything. It's odd, given how hard I rebelled against him myself. Not to speak of my left-of-center liberal-Democrat politics. What do I care about Ngo Dinh Diem?

At 3:30, we finish watching a movie called *Fly Away Home*. It's about a kid who learns to fly a plane so she can lead a flock of lost geese to Florida. My sister and mother and I all weep through the last half hour, and Dad smiles in perfect Buddhist happiness. When the credits roll, I smile at him. "You liked it," I say.

"*Loved* it," he says.

Then he sits across from me in his slippers and blue plaid pajamas, reading the paper. He doesn't want to take a nap. "At this point, I take nothing for granted," he whispers.

Halberstam, that asshole, trashed my old man again in 1971. This time, it was in an article for *Playboy*, and without the restraints imposed by the *Times*: "I did not think of J. R. as being a representative of a democracy. He was a private man, responsible to no constituency. Later, I was to think of him as being more representative of America than I wanted, in that he held power, manipulated it, had great money to spend—all virtually unchecked by the public eye. J. R., of course, bristled over the problems of working for a democracy. He disliked the press intensely. It was all too open. How could one counter communism, which was J. R.'s mission—little black tricks that never worked, lots of intelligence (mostly lies) coming in from his agents—with a free press?"

Aside from the line about countering communism, not one word of this pompous shit is true.

Dad can't take a dump. He goes to the bathroom and sits and sits, and it's really hurting him. My sister suggests that this is because he hasn't eaten for four days, so Dad weighs death against constipation and finally decides to drink a protein shake and some prune juice.

The next day, he's still constipated. He wants to go to the hospital, but then decides he doesn't want to go to the hospital even more, so he drinks another shake and more prune juice and starts vomiting almost constantly, spitting up a foul mixture of shake and prune juice and phlegm. Carrying the kidney-shaped dish to the bathroom, I gag and almost vomit myself. I'm starting to hate that infernal little Frankenstein pacemaker that keeps ticking his heart over and over, no matter what the rest of him wants and needs. I can see it under the mottled skin on his chest, hard and round like a hockey puck. Sometimes we joke about passing a magnet over it and putting him out of our misery. Dad nods out, forgets what he's saying, vomits again. Meanwhile, the TV news prattles on and on in the background like an evil guest who won't go away.

Once, I called the CIA public-information office and asked if I could see the old man's personnel records. CIA kids do stuff like this— one (who became a producer for *Unsolved Mysteries*) actually sued the agency under the Freedom of Information Act. A pleasant man named Dennis Klauer called me back with the official response: "Not only no, but hell no—and if you pursue this, we must contact John Richardson Sr. and remind him of his secrecy oath."

At around noon, he says he wants to have another talk, so we gather in the study, and he says pitifully, "My bowels have shut down."

The idiot blathering of CNN continues, distracting him for a moment.

"And something else—what else has shut down? My intestines?"

We turn the sound down and try again.

"Your lungs, you said."

"Yes."

Then the dog starts digging in the trash can, and my mom starts fretting, and my sister says she'll go get the garbage can from the guesthouse, because that one has a lid.

"I wish there was a lid for me," Dad says.

"That's pretty funny, Dad."

"Do you think there's a lid for me?" he asks.

I raise my hands to the heavens, taking the question for whimsy. But he persists.

"Do you think a doctor would do it?"

"What, Dad?"

He dips his head, his eyes going confidential. "Give me a lid for me."

It's odd how very old people get childlike when they tell a secret. For a second, I feel older than he is, and I lean forward and put my hand on his knee. "I don't think a doctor will," I say.

Then he nods so wearily that we try again to convince him to go to bed. But he won't. Never would, never will. Back in the binge days, I would see him walking to the kitchen at dawn with his tequila glass in hand. Sometimes he dropped it, and we would find the bloody footprints later. Now, when his hand droops, I try to pry loose the prune-juice glass without waking him, and he jerks back like I'm trying to steal it. Finally he drinks it down and I say, "As always, Dad, you drank it to the last drop." And I can't help feeling proud of him.

In the kitchen, my mother and I marvel over how tough he is. "It's a lesson in tenacity for me," I say. And she says, "It's a lesson for me that I won't go through that. I'll have my bottle of pills." And I put my hand on her neck and rub, and she shakes it off. "Don't do that!"

I went to his high school once, looked through his old yearbook. There was Richard Nixon looking like a young Richard Nixon. And there was Dad in a basketball uniform. He played on the varsity, never told me. The caption on the photo seems right to me even now: "Never flashy, but always in the thick of the battle, he proved in satisfactory manner to be a very capable guard."

Mom in bed. I say it's getting to be so hard on him. She says it's hard on us, too. Which is a sentiment worth honoring, I think. Weeping, she says she didn't think he'd wake up this morning, talks about maybe calling the doctor. A doctor put her friend Mary to sleep and would wake her up every few days to see if she was still in agony and finally just stopped feeding her through the tube. Maybe Mike would put a lid on him like he asked, put him in a deep sleep. Jennifer says the vet would be the best, and we laugh. And I think, Maybe it's up to me now. Maybe I should just do it and spare them the choice. So I go on the Internet and search for the Hemlock Society and discover it's all philosophy. "Where's the fucking how-to section!" I say.

Jennifer laughs. She's looking over my shoulder. "It's ridiculous," she says. "If you search for 'terrorist handbook,' they'll tell you how to make a pipe bomb."

"Maybe we can use a pipe bomb?"

"Might not work," she says. "He's pretty tough."

When I was twelve, the headmaster of my prep school wrote my dad a letter outlining my many flaws. I found it in my mother's papers a few years ago, furiously underlined by my old man: "His homework shows superficial, if any, preparation. He gives little thought to neatness or accuracy. He does not appear to possess the willingness to apply himself to the task at hand."

This morning, he finally took a dump. He feels much better. But he's so tired he didn't even watch the news, and when he goes to the bathroom again, he asks me to come in with him. Leaning on the edge of the sink, head hanging, he says very emphatically: "Remember—this—is—lung—cancer." When he's finished, I pull up his pants. I see his withered haunches. The pillow-damp hair is stuck wild to his head. But weak as he is, he still insists on washing his hands, leaning over the sink with his elbows on the tiles.

When I was thirteen, he took me on this trout-fishing trip to Nova Scotia. He was a big trout fisher when he was a young guy. I remember it as awkward and dull. We heard the same songs over and over on the radio: "Crimson and Clover," "I Think We're Alone Now," "Happy Together." He stopped the car a lot to pee—from booze, I assume.

I call home, and my youngest daughter says she's fallen in love with a book called *Ella Enchanted*. She loves it so much she took it to a slumber party and read it while the other girls watched the Spice Girls movie. I tell this to Dad. "That makes me very happy," he says. "I couldn't be happier. Tell her I said that."

He's peaceful tonight. Lies quietly, rises only to drink milk or medicine. Asleep at nine. I think the end is coming soon.

When I was fifteen, he started leaving books on my bed: *Waiting for Godot*, *The Trial*, Albert Camus's *Notebooks*. They changed my life, but we never discussed them. He just left them and never said a word.

In the bathroom, he sits on the toilet for twenty minutes. I sit in a plastic chair across from him. The bathroom is all yellow. There's a black-ink drawing of a rearing horse on the wall above him. I can tell he's thinking deeply about something, and finally he says it. "If—I—need—something, ask—your—mother—first. Because—we—have—the—past."

I want to be sure I know what he means. "If you need something specific, or anything?"

I have to repeat it a few times before he understands me.

"Anything," he finally says. "Because we have the past."

That night, I hear the nurse pounding on his back. He sits there gasping, head hanging, breathing the oxygen from the tubes. When he recovers, he says, "I can't take this anymore."

The nurse does everything she can to help him. It pisses me off. I point to the oxygen, to the pills. "*No esta bien; esta malo*," I say in my mangled Spanish: It's not good; it's bad. "*El necesita morir.*"

He needs to die.

At around four, he hisses out his frustration: "I—can't—die."

Looking at my father on his deathbed, I try to picture the romantic Berkeley boy who wore that "flowing, multicolored tie" and quoted Shelley. I'm so sorry I never met him. I used to be angry about it, but now I'm just sorry. And maybe a little bitter. And I don't know if Dad killed him out of shame or if he just held the knife straight while history pushed it in, but I do know that, as time passed, Dad replaced his doubts with convictions and became so absorbed in his war, he forgot that happiness was part of wisdom and that he owed it to himself and to his children to try and earn it. And that is a sad, sad thing. And a dangerous thing, too, because when you become too sure that life is a tragedy, then little by little you begin to accept tragedy, and finally something perverse in you even begins to invite it.

But life *is* a tragedy, isn't it?

One last trip to the bathroom. Even now, he won't use the bedpan. The toilet-paper roll is almost empty, and that's when he says his last words:

"Another roll."

I get one from the closet and hand it to him.

Back in his bedroom, he eases into sleep. As the dawn light rises in the window, his breathing starts to change. The agonizing long pauses when you think he's stopped, and then a gasp sucking the air back in for one more round. Long pause and gasp, long pause and gasp. It's horrible. There's something monstrous in those sucking gulps at air, something so hungry and automatic, like his self and will are just the creature of this tyrannical little spark of survivalist life that forces him to go on and on and on. Outside the birds are twittering and then the church bells ring as they do every morning here in Mexico, rolling out into the still, suspended air. Then Dad calms. His breathing gets softer and shallower breath by breath, with no more gasps or gulps, until he's breathing so peacefully, so gently, just skimming off the thin air at the top of his lungs. I move up and sit on the edge of the bed. The bells are finished, and now the garbage trucks rumble by.

The breaths get shorter and shorter and then he just stops.

The story you are about to read is true. Maybe. It involves a fugitive heiress, money, one very real gun, and layer upon layer of internet intimacy and digital deception. It's a mystery that takes place at the edge of technology, and a glimpse of the future we now inhabit—the birth throes of our uncertain world.

This is how she announced herself:

> **On March 2, 2003 at 4:12 pm, I disappeared. My name is isabella v., but it's not. I'm twenty something and I am an international fugitive.**

By that time, she said, she'd been on the run for a couple of weeks. The war in Iraq had just started and she was lonely. Maybe it was stupid to start a weblog, but that was better than the temptation to pick up the phone and call somebody from her old world. **In return, I suppose I have to keep you entertained. Keep you reading. That's the bargain. Keep your watchful eye on me—so that you might notice if I vanish suddenly. So that you might ask the questions that would save me.**

This appeared on BlogSpot, a pioneer in the online-diary form with a clever format that includes a hyperlink for reader responses. Eight people responded to that first cryptic post, ranging from sarcastic ("Saddam! Is this really you!") to lit crit: "The writing's a bit too Palahniuk—a little too obvious about trying to sound dramatic and cool."

But Isabella pressed on with another installment. "My family is an alarmingly influential pillar of a small European country," she began, drawing a family portrait that mixed *Masterpiece Theatre* with *The Godfather*. "Seventeen generations of fiscal conservatism. Seventeen generations of dynastic preservation and succession machinations. Seventeen generations of wealth accumulation.

Seventeen generations of primogeniture. Seventeen generations of sinister momentum."

It was heady stuff. "Is my father a mobster? No. Not in the conventional sense. Has my father had men killed? Women killed? Maybe."

Despite this . . . my father made four mistakes.
He gave birth to a redhead, and a daddy's little girl.
He sent me to the United States before I was 9.
He made me in his own image and taught me entirely too well . . . and then he arranged my marriage to Yves.

One evening, she logged on to muse about the risks of using false identification in the middle of a terrorist alert. "I'm going to buy a ticket tomorrow and head to my next waypoint if I can."

Maybe you were busy with war or making a living, but in the last few years the reality-and-illusion crowd has completely colonized the Internet. This isn't as trivial as it might seem. For thousands of years religious fanatics have been telling us that the physical world is an illusion and that we should focus on singing hymns or doing yoga. Now it's postmodern philosophers saying that reality is a matrix filled with invisible forests of signifiers best represented by obscure French and German words. On the net this translates to a giddy leap into the world of "immersive" games and anonymous transfer protocols that let forty-five-year-old men pretend to be thirteen-year-old girls. Which leaves you and me and the first guy to respond to Isabella's latest cliff-hanger all asking the same question:

Are you halfwits actually buying into this garbage?

Then Isabella posted again, this time a long and convincing description of the spycraft of escape—getting passports, draining bank accounts, hiding liquid assets (**particularly some loose diamonds I knew I could sell for local currency**), a life reduced to a laptop and a passport. **Moving feels safer for some reason. I only really feel secure when I'm on a plane.** Then she was in a warm and sunny place, studying books on how to disappear: **You have to actually become someone else. You have to be from somewhere.**

You have to have a history. Habits. Personality. Likes. Dislikes. You have to like cotton candy.

And on she went for another month and more than twenty-four thousand words, about how she found an underground money manager who helped her launder her trusts and came upon a blond man with eerie pale skin trying to force the door of her hotel room and dreamed about the same blond man sniffing her panties and about the long saga of her lonely girlhood at an elite private school and sneaking into her father's ornate library to pore through the stacks of books **until the light of the dawn in the window alerted me to the new day and I had to creep up to my room again.** She wrote about **the erotic allure of death** and about cutting herself on purpose **to leave something permanent on my body, as if to assert that I actually owned it and could do with it as I pleased.** She made references to Milan Kundera and Martin Scorsese and David Lynch and the ordinary people who **had school loans, car payments, credit card bills, mortgages, and designer groceries to carry.** She drew deft pictures of the strange town where **the flat light from overcast skies hurts my eyes** or the man blowing on his cappuccino, raising steam that **gives the impression that he is surrounded by his own personal microclimate.** She teased her readers with hints about dating on the run: **SWF, 20-something, flight risk with multiple identities seeks man of few words and fewer questions for semi-formal dating experiment. Risk of sudden disappearance must not be an obstacle.**

Whenever the story threatened to bog down, there was fresh adventure—she used an internet cafe and someone came around claiming to be her cousin, asking questions. **I ran and ran as fast as I could until I was completely out of breath.** Some of the most plummy writing was about her father and her fear of being committed to a mental institution, the **quiet wedding ceremony somewhere after which I'm committed somewhere with pink colored walls and progressive ideas about narcotics therapy. That breaks my big trust wide open and Yves and family take that and the dowry and recapitalize the business.** Then there was Alain, who arrived at her parents' house in a **motorcade of three sleek, black**

sedans filled with beautiful and elegant men in beautiful and elegant dark suits and gave her the **Montblanc Meisterstück pen** that changed her life shortly before he was **spectacularly murdered in the heart of Germany that late November day so long ago.**

By the middle of April, when winter was still hanging around like tuberculosis and the war was still going strong, a news blogger named Sean-Paul Kelley posted a story on agonist.org saying that "a major media outlet" was asking whether Isabella was real and a "former agent from Simon and Schuster" was sniffing around a book deal. Kelley had a spectacular amount of detail, speculating convincingly on who she might be—Paris Hilton? Liesel Pritzker?—and citing three sources: a mysterious security expert who said Isabella was very sophisticated about computer secrecy, a mysterious unnamed "friend of hers" who said he helped Isabella escape, and an unnamed attorney who was so mysterious he would hardly say anything at all. "If she is my client," he said, "I would hardly admit it to the media."

The next day, Kelley posted an update saying that "a source familiar with the family" told them that the family was thought to have hired either Pinkerton or Kroll, "the firm retained to track the assets of the Marcos fortune and Saddam Hussein in 1991." They wanted to handle this quietly.

On shes.aflightrisk.org Isabella responded immediately: **The news posted on The Agonist has got me to the point that I'm not going to get a wink of sleep (ever again?). What was confidence has melted into fear. I've been up I know not how long and I dare not go outside.**

By this time Isabella's readers had turned detective. Someone named "Tibbo" jumped on her clue about Alain's murder: **Considering the date and the place, the name Alfred Herrhausen comes to mind.** Herrhausen was a German banker killed in November 1989, by an extremely sophisticated bomb in one of Germany's most famous crimes. Someone else suggested she was from the **v. Finck family or maybe the Thurn and Taxis?** and someone named Jen responded: **The only thing about the von Fincks that I find intriguing is** that one of them is named Isabella v. She's Helmut's daughter and would be in her very early 20s now.

But other readers had softer hearts, like the one who told her to be strong. **You still have to go through the whole withdrawal, sorrow, angst, nervousness period. The first couple of years are the toughest. Keep writing. Be careful with valium. You can do this.** The next day LG sent a cheerful boost: **You write very well for someone who is sleep deprived!** And stella attacked the skeptics: **Some of the commentators here seem to be totally bereft of even a smidgen of compassion. For Isabella to have taken the risks she has taken, far beyond flight, it is a foregone conclusion that she must have had more than a few not so great reasons to motivate her to do so.**

The next day, Kelley posted a remarkable note on agonist.org:

FLIGHT RISK UPDATE

Earlier this week The Agonist received a cease-and-desist letter from an international law firm representing Isabella's family. For background, Isabella's Web log " . . . shes a flight risk" can be found here. In substance the letter demanded that The Agonist turn over any names or identifying information of sources for the Isabella story as well as remove any related material.

Kelley said he wasn't giving up the names and printed the letter, blacking out the names to protect the anonymity of Isabella and her family. The result looked like something out of an FBI file, all black stripes and threatening boilerplate, as if calculated to enflame the Isabella conspiracy theorists. **It has come to our attention that certain unauthorized and libelous disclosures ....**

Someday there will be Internet epidemiologists, and this could be one of the classic case studies on how a mind virus spreads. As May began, someone named "darklytr" posted a note to a website called Collective Detective: **Whaddaya think? Fact or fiction?** A few of the collective detectives followed the links and came back skeptical, but things were quiet until Isabella jumped in. **No, I am not writing a screen play. I have turned down five interview requests. I have been offered three book deals. I have accepted none.**

Her arrogant tone hit the skeptics like a rock in a wasps' nest. **Let's see,** said Cortana. **You started a weblog despite the fact that you are a self-proclaimed fugitive and wanting to start over? No better way to do that than to write about . . . wait for it . . . wait for it . . . YOUR PAST! That thing that you want to forget.**

In the next phase the virus jumped borders with an article on Wired News by a writer named Leander Kahney with hyperlinks to the dozens of weblogs which by now were debating the reality of Isabella. There were "tantalizing clues" like an "IP address in the Bahamas" and the oddity of Isabella's emails—he'd corresponded with her himself, in fact. And there was a New York literary agent named Bob Mecoy who said he was ready to represent Isabella even if she didn't exist: "Though it's a better story if it's true, it doesn't necessarily matter. If it turns out not to be, I'll pitch Isabella as a fiction writer."

The list of believers grew. Early in May, someone calling himself "terr-am-ater" posted the results of his research into her domain registration:

> **AeroBeta, Sociedad Anonima**
> **Apartado Postal 0832-0387**
> **World Trade Center**
> **Panama, Republica de Panama WTC**

A few hours later, "anonymous coward" developed the point. **Someone spent several thousand dollars to set up a careful structure. that seems an elaborate effort for a hoax. too many details point away from the hoax theory for my taste.** And he decoded the company name:

aero = flight
beta = a financial measure of risk.
AeroBeta, s.a. = flight risk, s.a.

Do a little research, he taunted. **It would be interesting to know how much of a link there is between "fiction" theory types and basic laziness.**

Then someone calling himself BuddhaG made a pitch for Isabella as a new form of art: **You would have been one of those jerks that said Joyce was garbage too probably, until he got read by enough people. Until somebody put it in a nice frame for you. Or that Picasso or Jackson Pollack didn't know how to paint because what they painted didn't look like anything.** The way he saw it, the whole Isabella phenomenon **could end up saying something about the nature of our perception of truth. It could say something about how we understand and perceive information.**

It got ugly after that. Maybe there was nowhere else to go but down. When "mistik" arrived to say Isabella was real, someone else accused him of being a plant. As it happened, he wasn't the only Isabella defender who was "spoofing"—hijacking someone's email address to send untraceable messages, routing the emails through taunting fronts like twomirrorsfacing@mail.com. But mistik came back just as strong. **Of course my identity, location, info etc is completely spoofed. I do that as standard practice on the internet. It is irrelevant to the exploration of the Isabella mystery.**

By this time, I am corresponding with Isabella myself. My first note is: **I'm a reporter from Esquire. I'd love to chat by email,** ending with: **Come on, Isabella. Why not?**

This is what I get back:

First off, don't goad me. It is unseemly for a professional and makes me wonder if you don't have an ulterior motive. I'm only responding because I liked your piece "I, Stalkerazzi" and because I'm tired of getting emails from people you have

approached for attributable comments asking me "what is his deal?" Second, if you are actually John Richardson of Esquire and you have a legitimate media interest in an interview I will consider it under very strict conditions.

The conditions include calling her attorney in Panama. **Mr Ceaser is hard to reach. This is not accidental. If you are interested enough to be persistent you will get a hold of him. If not I have little interest in talking with you. Right off the bat I can tell you that we will require editorial control on the final article.**

She's awfully haughty for a person who probably doesn't even exist.

Hi Isabella,

Thanks so much for writing. And I'm thrilled that you liked Stalkerazzi. It's one of my personal favorites. Blah blah blah . . . but there's one thing I can't agree to, and that's editorial control of my final article. If you check with your advisors, they'll tell you that no legitimate publication (at least in the United States) lets a subject see a piece before it's printed. It's actually a firing offense, as TK found out in Vanity Fair a few years ago.

But I hit send too fast and have to write a quick follow-up to explain that editors use "TK" for "to come" and I stuck it there because I couldn't remember the name of the *Vanity Fair* reporter. **I'm doing too many things at once.** In her next email, she informs me that everything we are writing is off the record and makes fun of my little mistake:

Met with "Isabella" today in the TK climes of TK. She is about TK tall and weighs around TK and her hair is TK. Surprisingly, I have discovered that she is actually Ms. TK and is traveling under the name of TK. She is a woman of TK, TK and TK. I am in the process of finishing out the article based on my interview and should have it done by TK.

I write back.

Don't be so cynical.

Actually, I like that. Ms. TK.

She could go on a date with Mr. Re.

She writes back.

Better that she marry Mr. O. Then she'd be Mrs. TK-O.
Later she posted an entry on her blog under the title "TK."

So Isabella and I are collaborating on an interactive fiction. Or is it some kind of immersive game? Maybe all the circuitry humming in the background makes you fall into some kind of digital swoon, but I can't stop myself from musing on the meaning of it all, our religious need to fill the emptiness of the internet with a more perfect version of ourselves. Or some such nonsense. But it really comes down to this: Isabella is almost certainly some fat-assed internet loser, and the loser on the other end of the modem is me.

Now it is my goal to charm her. So I tease her about being hypersensitive and she writes me a reply in the middle of the night. **I only come off Hypersensitive. I do seem much more abrasive in email than in person I am told.** Then she demands "editorial control" again and brings up the embedded reporters in Iraq and bristles when I promise to be fair. **That's a subjective and bullshit term bandied about by media types to mean whatever suits them that day. Don't feed me that line. It's not going to be fair if I get caught.** In fact, unless I state in my next email that all discussions so far and in the future were in fact off the record, then **it will be the last you hear from me and I will group you in the "slimy reporters" bin.**

After cooling down, I make another attempt to break through. **It's late. I'm tired. It's been a rough week. I got illness in the family and relationship issues and you're driving me crazy. Would it kill you to be just a tiny bit more cooperative? Okay, maybe that wasn't the best phrasing.** She writes back and says she's sorry I'm having a hard time but it's tough all over and this is my last chance. **I am running potentially for my life. I'm not having a real good time either.**

Finally I just give in. **Okay, to hell with it—these negotiations are off the record. Let's move to the next level.** But I don't want to be another phony in a phony world so I also tell her I am feeling very uncomfortable. **I know that many clever people think there is no truth and therefore nothing to trust. But I do not believe**

**this. I find it glib and sophomoric. So let me be perfectly clear—
if this is a spoof and you are negotiating in bad faith, I won't
feel bound by this agreement or any other.**

I begin autodialing Panama, talking in *muy malo español* to a very
impatient receptionist. After about a week I finally reach Mr.
Carlos Ceaser. Yes, he says, although he advised against it, Isabella is
willing to do interviews under certain strict limitations. If I would
email him a list of questions, he would respond with a list of their
requirements.

Then I don't hear from either one of them for a week. When I get
through to Ceaser again, he says he's waiting for instructions.

Another week. Then she writes me again, apologizing, saying
she's been going through a hard time. Swinging for the fences, trying
to work the game on all levels and be honest at the same time, I tell
her a wild story that happens to be true:

**A couple of weeks ago, I met this girl on the Internet. She had
read my last book, which is about dwarfs and has a lot of stuff
in it about body image and beauty. So we started talking about
families and difference and stuff and little by little we become
more personal and intimate, as one does on the internet. And
after a while I wanted to see what she looked like. But she
wasn't comfortable with it. She wanted to have a relationship
without looks involved. I began to think that maybe she was
a dwarf herself and maybe she was fucking with me as some
kind of dwarf revenge. One day she mentioned her picture
appearing in a newspaper so I did a search and turned up the
article and called the paper and had them mail it to me. But
here's the thing—in the week it took to arrive, I became so close
to this invisible woman that when the envelope came, my heart
started to pound. I wasn't sure I wanted to open it and kill the
fantasy. And it felt like I was violating her trust, her expressed
request not to involve our physical persons. On the other hand,
I didn't want to develop feelings for some pretend person. I like
bodies. I like the physical world. I'm not into fantasy novels or**

fantasy movies or religious fairy stories either. So the envelope sat there at my desk all day. At ten that night, I called her and asked if she was ready to send me a picture. She said she was. So I told her about the envelope. She felt violated at first but calmed down when I pointed out that I hadn't opened it. And finally she told me to open it. And I ripped it open and looked at her face for the first time.

I want to talk to you on the phone.

In response, Isabella gives me Bob Mecoy's phone number and says he's acting as her literary agent. And minutes later I'm speaking to an actual real person. But minutes after that it becomes clear that Mecoy has never actually spoken to Isabella, only communicated with her by email. He's hoping *I'll* find out the truth. "Like you, I want to press the flesh," he says. "I wanna see the high school yearbook."

Another week goes by. Then another. Finally Mecoy calls. "What are you doing the nineteenth?"

Meeting Isabella?

She's agreed to my compromise on editorial review, correcting the transcript of our interview instead of the story itself. Her security will be contacting me by phone. I'll fly to a major airport and get instructions to drive to a secure location where heavily armed security will meet me, strip-search me, and take me by small plane or car to a more secure location. No recording devices or cameras and after a two-hour interview I will have to remain in place until a "distance barrier" is established.

I send my editor an email: **I'm starting to believe. But it still could be the wild goose chase of all time.**

Later Mecoy follows up with a memo repeating all the points above, ending with a flourish that's pure Isabella: **Please be aware that this interview is expensive (these security measures are costing her in excess of $20,000), risky and inconvenient. She is accepting your assurances that this is a serious interview and will be quite upset if you are, as she says, "playing games."**

I wrote a story about a con "artist" once, a scumbag who made $90 million selling shares in the life insurance policies of terminally ill patients who existed only in his imagination. He sued me on his way to being indicted. One thing I learned from that lovely experience is that hustlers always accuse *you* of conning *them*. It's a way of getting you off-balance. And maybe on some level they believe it and use it to justify all the nasty things they do. So I've never been amused by the thin line between reality and illusion and never really got why artists and philosophers think it's so damn interesting. It's *annoying*. Getting things right is hard work. You have to stop clicking and cutting and get out the yellow marker. Because rational thought is sequential, like Marshall McLuhan said. And now that I'm running my emails through an encryption technology called Hushmail, the runaway heiress is giving answers that must be studied:

My mother hasn't been much the subject of my writings because she was always on my side. I haven't wanted to subject her to dark scrutiny. She's just a woman in the last vestige of truly male dominated enclaves. My father openly has mistresses, etc. She enjoys her role in many ways as a power wife and a charity socialite, but she always wanted a bit more. She talks about childhood among the superrich, the **huge hall at home, with portraits of all our relatives going back to like 1120. My Great-great-great-whatever Uncle's suit of armor he fought in the Crusades with is on display.** She describes in detail the point when it began to dawn on her that the money and the cars and the planes weren't freedom but a method of control. **Didn't like how I was behaving? Take away access to the jet. Not riding enough dressage? Turn off the cash spigot. Instant contrite and proper daughter.**

But I just can't connect with her. In other internet relationships I've learned that you have to fill in for all the missing physical cues with glimpses of your daily life and emotional reactions, so I mention that I was also raised by servants and sent to an elite private school, things you might think a lonely person on the run might use to start a personal conversation. But Isabella stays cool and professional. Periodically she copies our email strings to Mecoy.

And she never writes on weekends.

On July 9, I open my Hushmail account and find this:
Make plans for a flight to:
Las Vegas
El Paso
Seattle
San Juan, Puerto Rico

Well, this is progress. Maybe I was wrong, maybe she just seemed cold because she was a reserved person, like Meryl Streep in *A Cry in the Dark*. My office puts holds on tickets for all four places, and more and more I begin to believe in her, if only because it would seem rude to be talking to someone and not believe in them a little.

I was pretty introverted as a girl. I read a lot. I hatched grand conspiracies. That sort of thing.

. . . I don't have ALL that much respect for my brothers. I don't really have any clue what they "want" other than to spend money and sleep with women. Very aristo.

. . . For years I had an American Express platinum card that some guy with a green eyeshade in a basement somewhere just paid the bill for. I never even knew how much I had put on it. It always seemed to get paid regardless. (I tried to find the ceiling once, and failed.) I think I had refused to come home or something when I was like 17 or 18 and suddenly the card was turned off. I was stranded in Scandinavia and had to call home to get back—and then was forced to attend the social event I had been avoiding. That was alarming.

. . . If "Alain" could be gotten to, so could anyone. My father had upset quite a lot of people with his corporate and banking endeavors. (He was on both the Arab and the Jewish blacklists at the same time at one point.)

. . . I spent a lot of time sneaking into night clubs, trying to be more exposed to "teen socialization" and the rituals thereof. I was really far too cold, too reserved to be a very good girlfriend, I expect. I suppose I might have been considered good "fling"

material. If you liked the elven look then you probably found me attractive. Charlie Brown's "Little Redheaded Girl." "That's the rich girl . . . with the red hair. Her dad owns jets."

. . . I had spent all this time in High School and beyond going wherever I pleased, doing whatever I wanted. Traveling to France in the middle of the school year. That sort of thing. No one seemed even vaguely interested until later. Instead of gaining independence with the arrival of 20-something I was losing it.

. . . You don't send your kid to the center of the free world, take a two decade long hands-off approach to child rearing, allow them to make associations, friends, and become culturally attuned to that place during their most formative years, open a financial spigot so large that it would be impossible to drink from it without spilling, express nearly no interest in the choices and travels of this child and then, suddenly, reverse yourself when they are at their most independent and expect to be able to exert unopposed control—that is, unless you are my father.

. . . My mother has done a brilliant job of finding her path through this noise. She does it primarily by realizing and cultivating her access to my father and his aides. Though she is a European wife, no aide would dare tell her "no" to anything. And she holds considerable sway over my father. She is often a soft voice. She tends to breathe warmth into his actions—which would otherwise seem cold and sterile. Most importantly, she understands him. I think she is quite satisfied to play this role. I used to catch her smiling to herself when she had persuaded him to do something he was otherwise uninclined to. Her view, I'm sure, was that I could become like her. The power behind the scenes. "Who could you ever marry that you would not lead by the nose with a string. . . . " she asked me once.

. . . My sex life is mostly uninteresting. I've only had 3 serious relationships, by serious I mean with a sexual component. I think what you mean is that Yves was/is an attempt to get my sexual exploits "back in line" with expectations. Unfortunately,

I never had enough to be "out of line" with expectations. There was one incident where a smitten boy stalked me (back before stalking was a big deal) and had a decidedly unpleasant run-in with security people. (Spent the night in jail with a broken nose when he mouthed off to one I guess.)

... I was just stunned by the credit card thing. At first it was played off like there was a problem of some kind but if I came home it would all be fixed. It was only later that I found out it was by design.

... How did I react? I spent a lot of time quietly thinking about it. Planning. I realized that every place I went, every dollar I spent was being watched. I started using more cash, being more careful. The more careful I was the more I realized the depth of control my father had. The more I realized how much I had been giving away. I stopped giving it away.

... Live your whole life with infinite freedom, so free you are constantly bored because there is no challenge in life. None. Want something? Make a phone call. Don't like it? Hand it back, another one appears. Curious what Lynda is doing in Nice? Get on the Concorde to Paris and fly to Nice that afternoon. Slowly discover that there might be some challenges for you in the corporate world. That, indeed, money is not the only reward there. (Indeed, it better not be, because I had more of that than I knew what to do with.) Start exploring your options, slowly, carefully. Get excited for the first time in a long while. Then, suddenly, have it taken away and a very obvious prison put in its place.

At 2:32 on the afternoon of July 14, my phone rings and a man's voice comes on, crackling with cell static and sounding vaguely official. He says he's on Isabella's security team and I can call him David. "I'm trying to understand why a face-to-face meeting is to her advantage, and frankly I'm having a hard time." But he tells me to be ready to go to Las Vegas or San Juan. He'll give me twenty-four hours notice. "Expect brutal sun," he says.

Then the deadline arrives and I still haven't heard from them. I send her an email:

Well, Isabella . . . it's time. What's going on?

Friday morning David calls again. "The location will be Las Vegas. Rent a car and email a description of the car and the hotel and wait for further instructions."

A few minutes later, he calls back to ask if I have a valid passport.

Then I call the travel agent and book the ticket, the hotel, the car.

He calls again at six. The meeting is going to be pushed forward a day—or canceled. I tell him my ticket is nonrefundable. "Should I get on the plane or not?"

I would wait, he says.

That night, Mecoy gets a message encrypted through an anonymizer in Liechtenstein. It came from a guy he's written to before, supposedly a friend of Isabella's. "He said she and her security people have been separated," he tells me the next morning, "and they believe she's been snatched."

Snatched? You've got to be kidding me.

That was his reaction, too, he tells me. So he shot an email right back at the guy asking **Who are you?** and **Who is she?** and **What is going on?!** And then the phone rang and it was the guy and he said someone from the security team called him in the middle of the night asking if he knew where she was. They couldn't find her and they thought she'd been snatched. But he always told her to build some sort of "dead-man trigger," some envelope to the authorities or message that would pop up on her website within forty-eight hours of her abduction. Later the mystery man calls again and says the reason nobody called to cancel my meeting is because they felt it was too much of a coincidence—"They're setting up a meeting with you and she gets taken."

What? Some security service tapped the phone of a reporter? Listened twenty-four hours a day to my boring conversations so they could track down a blogging heiress? It's ridiculous.

"I may have had my fly unzipped," Mecoy says, sounding a little embarrassed.

A few days later I tell the whole crazy saga to an ex-Navy Seal who protects presidents and he cuts me off after about two minutes. "I don't even have to think about it—it's 100 percent fucking con."

Then David calls again. But I've given up on her. Game over. He says he wants to explain. There was an attempt to "repatriate her." There was gunfire. Will I meet him in San Francisco? He promises to have some kind of proof that will make it all worthwhile—but of course he can't tell me on the phone.

So here I am in California, sitting like a putz next to the phone. The hotel TV says another kid just got blown up in Iraq and I turn it off. Maybe it's time to reconsider this whole journalism deal, this business of letting things happen and taking notes. It makes you feel like an eternal ten-year-old, waiting for Dad to honk the car horn.

Then the phone rings. "The meeting is on," David says. "I'll call you again at 5:45 and give you details."

"Where is it going to be?"

"I'll tell you at 5:45."

Just after 5:30, the phone rings again. "Can you be at the Ritz-Carlton at 5:45?"

"I don't know. Where's the Ritz-Carlton?"

"Two blocks away."

"Then I can be there."

"Go to the reception desk and tell them you have a meeting with Mr. Smith."

Sure, fine. And if the Ritz-Carlton clerk doesn't give me a blank stare, he'll point me to some dandruff-trailing geek at the bar who will tell me that it was all just a "fiction" just before I punch him in the nose. But I stuff a tape recorder and a camera into my backpack and walk down California Street.

And there's the Ritz. Damn, it's a palace. The doormen are wearing black top hats. The lobby has that muffled-by-money hush. And when I mention Mr. Smith, the clerk blooms into a warm smile. "Hello, Mr. Richardson," she says, and waves over a bellman who guides me to what seems like a private elevator bank and slides a magnetic card into a slot, pressing the number for the top floor. "Will you be all right or would you like to be escorted?"

"I'll be all right."

Up I go and out the door and down the hall to the very end. The carpet is thick, the door solid.

Knock-knock.

"When I open the door," a male voice says, "wait for a count of five and then enter."

After a moment someone unlatches the door and leaves it propped open on the brass tongue. But I forget my instructions. "Am I going to count to five or are you going to count to five?"

No answer. So one two three four five and push open the door . . .

I have plenty of time to take in my surroundings, to note the single white orchid on the coffee table and the Dell laptop open on the desk. The bed in the other room is rumpled. And there's a man with a very big gun—a black assault rifle that looks very modern and high-tech. He's pointing it at the floor at a curious angle and my mind goes into one of those dreamlike blurs that take over when you get into an accident or a fight.

The man throws something metal at my feet. In a soothing and courteous voice, he says they're handcuffs and he's very sorry but he's going to have to ask me to put them on. It's procedure.

I look down and it's like a shot in a movie: CLOSE-UP on police cuffs. They shine like mercury. They look heavy. "That's not going to happen," I say.

"Then you'll have to sit down and let me search you."

"Fine. No problem. Search away."

He's strikingly handsome and very well dressed—dark suit, fancy loafers, French cuffs. Some kind of ethnic blood gave him brown skin and Elvis-black hair, Filipino maybe. "You're David?"

He nods. "Obviously that's not my real name." Then he tells me to empty my backpack of all tape recorders, cameras, pens, and other metal objects. I can use one pen to write but best not make any sudden movements. Then he mutters into his earpiece microphone and takes a stance in the doorway to the bedroom with his weapon pointing diagonally at the floor.

"What kind of a gun is that?"

"A Bushmaster AR-15."

A minute or two passes and then the door opens behind me. David holds his stance. I twist in my chair to see.

Close to the root of faith, there is a longing for the blissful mindless days before we ate of the fruit of knowledge and saw that we were naked and were ashamed. On the other side are the modernists and perverts who say we should take ambiguity as a challenge and invent the future as we go along. But both sides agree with this: The minute we put names to things, we stepped into a symbolic world where nothing would ever be fixed and solid—where we are haunted by words, the ghosts of real things.

Reading this story, you're still in that symbolic world. But I'm not. I've stepped through the looking glass. *This is real.*

She's thin and pale, with significant hollows scalloped under her eyes and fine hair that orangey color you get when you try to go blond but don't quite make it. About five-seven, slender, and elegant in black heels and black pants and a white top. Isabella sits in the armchair at the other end of the coffee table.

"Are you surprised?"

Hell yes, I'm surprised. But it still feels like I'm gliding on magnetic rails. Could be an actress. A hunk with a carbine. Directed by Michael Mann.

She gives me a nervous smile, tells me to ask questions, but I just don't know what to say. How you doing? Seen any good movies lately? Have you noticed that guy standing there *with that gigantic fucking gun?* Finally I just blurt out the last thought to rattle across my brainpan, that she looks tired, and she says she was shot at so yes she's tired and scared too. So I ask why her father would have someone shoot at her and she says it's all a bit confusing, maybe it wasn't her father at all, just some random thing. Then she looks up at David and he says he's sorry but all they can really say at this time is that two bullets hit the car, one whizzing through the air in front of her and the other passing through the seat cushion under her legs.

"It just seems insane," I say.

"It is insane," she answers. "But I wouldn't put anything past my father."

Then she tells me about being on the run and always having security around and having to plan each move and feeling like she's traded one prison for the next. Half of the wild loops on my pad won't make any sense later. But slowly she starts to make sense. When she says it's exciting to defy her father, the light flashes in her eyes. I'm getting more used to her rhythms, from girlish hesitation to aloof poise to these sudden sunbursts of energy. Emotions move quickly across her face but she's restrained, an attractive quality. She's nervous and also a little imperious. And she's actually quite fine and beautiful. So maybe she still doesn't have good answers for all my questions—the reason she doesn't just hold a press conference is because she still feels some family loyalty despite the arranged marriage and relentless hunt and possible murder attempt—but now all the lousy answers seem to fit together. "I'm thinking the weblog was a mistake," she says. "It seemed like a release, an outlet, a kind of a game . . ."

She stops and grins. "But I've grown to like it a lot. It's drawn quite an audience. It puts me out there, but it's safe. It's disguised."

"Do you ever think your parents might read it?"

"I've fantasized about that—look what I've done!"

And it lights up her face. And suddenly I like her and I want to help her. What exactly does she want from me? What am I doing here?

"I want people *to believe that I'm real*," she says. Then she gives a little laugh. "I've felt a little unreal—like a ghost. It feels a little narcissistic, to put myself out there—but I *want* to."

How much time had gone by? Half an hour? An hour? I can't tell you. That Dell laptop on the desk must be the Latitude C400 she mentions in her blog, the one that runs Debian and uses AirSnort. Hold that up to the suits of armor and the seventeen centuries of sinister momentum and it all makes sense. It's a modern story and she's a modern girl trapped between the past and the future, trying to break out for a little run of freedom. And the internet dream state is not just a vast slump of losers dreaming away in their pods; it's the digital confessional, where people drop their guard and explore their fantasies and make swift and deep connections in the anarcho-syndicalist hive where we are dreaming the future. And Isabella's talking about hiding in the shadows and trying to look bored and never knowing how much she can tell people—or say, a guy—when suddenly she stops. "I'm close to tears right now. I haven't talked to anyone except security for so long, I don't know what I can say anymore."

"Do you want a moment to compose yourself?" David asks.

She says she does and walks past him to the bathroom. This has the feeling of something rehearsed. He holds his stance but says he's sorry for misleading me with the thing about getting snatched, and I realize that it is getting very hot and stuffy in this room. Doubtless air conditioning would interfere with their sophisticated counterspy gadgets.

A minute later she comes back. "I'm more composed now," she says with a nervous laugh. We talk for another hour or so. Sometimes she looks to David, who responds in a soothing and measured voice somewhere between Secret Service man and camp counselor. Several times she says she's feeling more relaxed, and once when David interrupts to tell her to be careful, she teases him. "David is more controlling than my father was."

"But better looking," I say.

She laughs. "He doesn't like it when I flirt with him, and he doesn't have a sense of humor." She looks down her nose at the Bushmaster. "I want to know if that thing is really necessary—that's what you should ask him."

David acts somber. "If I shoot them, I want them to go down the first time."

We are playing parts, of course. She's bringing a touch of Audrey Hepburn to the whole girl-in-jeopardy thing, David's doing some kinda Gary Cooper G-man, and I'm the barefoot reporter oozing human sympathy like a slug. Some of it is true and some we're laying on just to keep things coherent, adding yet another layer of confusion to this modern dilemma of identity.

Which brings us to Yves, her bridegroom. They grew up together, she says. She even had a crush on him. And then one night out of the blue her family and his family went to dinner and the two fathers started talking about a trust fund and a dowry and at first she thought they were talking about some other couple—and then it hit her. And then it hit Yves. "He got up and walked away, and I started crying. There I was, rejected already even before I was a bride. He did not want it at all. And it was very clear that I would only be the wife, never the lover, never the desired—and I will only marry for love."

She'll never understand why her father was not "amenable to argument." It wasn't like the families were a particularly good business match or anything. She couldn't figure it out. She almost felt something was being kept from her. And even now she sometimes thinks she's just acting like a spoiled rich girl and if Yves hadn't bolted from the table maybe she would have tried to make it work— but why would her father want to marry her to a guy who was going to treat her like shit for fifty years?

"Careful," David says.

But the subject makes her emotional, turning her mind to all the things she has lost. "I felt at home at home," she says. "I knew my position. I knew who I was. I knew what I wanted."

A bit later, she stops. "I actually feel very exposed right now."

A few minutes after that, she ends the interview.

I sit and scribble. David holds his stance in the bedroom doorway and talks on his earset. "Extract One . . . all right, sounds good . . . clear One." Then he heaves a big sigh and unslings the Bushmaster AR-15 and opens his jacket and pours himself a glass of Pellegrino from the big green bottle on the table. It's hard work holding a gun like that on your feet for two solid hours. Relaxing, working the muscles in his shoulders, he tells me he got his start "some years ago" in counternarcotics work somewhere in Latin America and researched this carefully before getting involved. What tipped it was her family, how ruthless they were. That's not how families are supposed to behave. In the first few months on the run, they found a bug at least once and had to blow town a couple of times when the searchers got too close. They "chronically underestimated" the search effort. Fortunately Isabella had resources of her own—tens of millions, which was good because the team was expensive and they couldn't fly commercial anymore. This trip alone cost $75,000. Eventually they would have to find a way to stabilize the situation.

He wants me to know that Isabella is fragile. She has nightmares, lots of stuff about being chased and not being able to run fast enough. She probably couldn't survive without money. She doesn't know how to have relationships, to flirt and be normal. But she is not a bird you can keep in a cage. Even after her blog cost her two lawyers, she still kept publishing the damn thing. And being her security man was no picnic either. "She's this post-adolescent redhead," he says with a meaningful shrug. "It gets tough."

At this point I notice the lovely cuff links with pale-blue oval stones. He's wearing Zegna, Zanella, and Gucci loafers. The eurotexture shirt is particularly stylish. "How do I know you're not just her boyfriend posing with a gun and there's just the two of you and no security team at all?"

He smiles like this is the most ridiculous thing I've said yet, and pops a bullet out of the chamber of his rifle. "Want a souvenir?" he asks. It's a .223 fifty-five-grain full metal jacket, about two inches long.

As I walk out through the hushed lobby a moment later, the friendly clerk says, "Goodbye, Mr. Richardson." It's dark out now and chilled by a fog so thick it makes my face wet. Later the doubts will come back—an assault rifle at the Ritz-Carlton? Who really wrote that threatening letter to agonist.org? Couldn't a big-time lawyer solve all this with one phone call? In a week I'll ask her to let me call her parents for comment, setting off an ugly episode of suspicion and hostility. But that all comes when I step back out of my body and get back to the world of symbols, safe at my computer, and it will never feel as true and alive as this moment right now, walking through the misty chilled streets with the city lights turning the fog gold. I was wrong to be so cynical. Sometimes you really do make a connection and rise to the level of your dreams.

Isabella is real.

I think.

She still writes to me, telling me about landing strips in the middle of nowhere and sitting in a charming open-air room on an island known for its beaches. She talks about melting into the world and the wonderful moment when the rain breaks. I check my Hushmail account every day.

There's my plane, she says today. **Gotta go.**

I SHOULD HAVE BEEN THERE TO PROTECT HIM:

THE INTIMATE STORY OF MICHAEL BROWN SR. AND THE AGONY OF THE BLACK FATHER IN AMERICA

On Monday, Michael Brown Sr. will be attending the funeral of his son, who was gunned down by a police officer in Ferguson, Missouri and left bleeding in the street for more than four hours. Amidst the tumult of demonstrations, he's calling for the protesters to be peaceful. His wife tells him, "You can't call for peace looking like you want to hurt somebody."
The problem is, he does.

It is Thanksgiving at Mike Brown's house, three days after a grand jury declined to bring charges against the policeman who killed his son and his city exploded in riots. His wife, Calvina, and her mother and various daughters and sisters and cousins bustle around the kitchen preparing the feast. The men gather downstairs in the man cave, watching the Eagles school the Cowboys. Because they're Americans and this is the day Americans consecrate to gratitude, the Brown family tries to stick to easy topics—food, sports, music, children, absent relatives—everything but the nightmare that has changed their lives forever. Soon they will take their places around the table. Soon they will bow their heads and pray. Soon they will declare the things that still make them, despite everything, thankful.

Brown's house is an ordinary ranch in a pleasant, safe neighborhood a few miles from where his son was killed, completely average except for one thing—down in the man cave the walls are decorated with photos of Brown's dead son, a tapestry of his dead son, a photo of a mural dedicated to his dead son. Hanging on the corner of the TV is a black necktie with his dead son's face peeking out at the very bottom, like a bit of sun under a long black cloud. Brown leans against a pillow bearing his dead son's face. Mike-Mike, they called him, as if saying his name once weren't enough to express their love.

Brown is a tall, powerfully built man with a shaved head and a handsome face that seems perpetually solemn. In the months since his son died, he's stopped cutting his beard, which makes him look like a figure from the Old Testament. As always, he's wearing a T-shirt bearing his dead son's face. He just got back from an overnight trip to New York, where he did five TV interviews in one day, and he looks exhausted but also relieved. The tension is over, the faint hope of a conviction extinguished, and now the real struggle begins. He leans back into the sofa and tries to relax, tapping ashes from a Newport into a red plastic cup.

Downstairs, the men make a real effort to focus on the game, but in the absence of women and children the conversation turns to the big subject: the protests all across the country, the gratifyingly widespread criticism of the prosecutor and his tactics, the news coming out about how the Ferguson authorities bungled the crime-scene investigation by failing to measure the distance between shooter and victim, failing to record the first interview with the officer, failing to take his gun away at the scene, failing to prevent him from washing his hands, the medical examiner who couldn't be bothered to replace a dead camera battery—a series of errors so relentless it's hard to believe they weren't screwing up things on purpose.

And the thing his son's killer said about feeling like a five-year-old fighting Hulk Hogan? "He was six four," Brown says. "So now they're saying Mike-Mike was six six. He was six four. Just had a little more weight on him, and most of it was flab."

Kids run in and out, and the men change the subject. Cal's mom comes down to smoke a cigarette, taking off a shoe to rub her foot over her tiny toy poodle. Brown goes upstairs and comes back with his baby daughter on his arm, dressed in a holiday dress and pretty shoes. He props her on the cushion and she stares ahead with a sleepy, solemn face. Then Rev. DeVes Toon of Al Sharpton's National Action Network arrives with an uncle of Oscar Grant's—the man whose death at the hands of a California police officer was memorialized in the movie *Fruitvale Station*—and he describes his latest idea for a publicity campaign: pictures of families at their Thanksgiving tables with one seat empty, propping up a picture of their lost child. "You gotta keep the heat on them," he says. Through peaceful means, he adds, although he believes the officer who killed his nephew never would have been convicted if not for the riots that followed his death. "In the back of their minds, they gotta smell the smoke. You know what I'm saying?"

Brown listens but doesn't respond. Soon the conversation shifts to yesterday's interviews. Of course they all wanted to know how it feels. The lawyers have been telling him to open up, so that's what he tried to do. But some of it's just weird, like pretending to walk down the hall so they can get some B-roll footage.

"Like acting?"

He laughs. "That's what I've been doing for the last three months—acting, acting, acting."

Here, with his family and friends, he seems almost like a different person—quiet as usual, but less so, comfortable in his den, the regular guy he was before his life became a public nightmare.

It begins on a Saturday, August 9. Brown gets a call at his mother-in-law's house around lunchtime. Mike-Mike is lying in the street out on Canfield Drive, dead.

Brown runs out to his car, with Cal chasing after him. He's sure it's a mistake—it has to be a mistake. He and Cal just got married three weeks ago and Michael was his best man, grinning nonstop in his rented suit. How could he be dead?

Ten awful minutes in a hot metal box. As they approach the shooting site, traffic blocks their way. They leave the car and run. Another car door flies open and out jumps Michael's mother, Lesley McSpadden. On Canfield Drive, where a housing complex begins, a series of modest two-story apartment buildings, they see police cars and yellow tape and a growing crowd.

In the middle of the street, a body lies covered by a sheet. Brown scans the crowd and Michael isn't there, and people tell him that really is his body under the sheet. But a voice in his head keeps saying, *No, that's not him. Can't be true.*

He just cannot take it in. His mind pushes it away. *I should have been there to protect him*, he thinks. The time the cop asked for Michael's ID when he was standing on the front porch, when he was ten years old and so big he already looked like a man, Brown told the officer, "Officer, that boy is a minor, so you better talk to me." When Michael was sixteen, they had the talk about being cooperative with police. "It's not a bow-down thing," Brown said. "They just have things they have to do." And just a few months ago, his son told him the police were always messing with people on Canfield, saying stuff as they walked down the street. Brown said, "Well, what do you say back?" Michael said, "Nothing. I just keep walking."

Brown goes up to a police officer and tells him he's the father, asking if he can identify the body—he has to see it with his own eyes. He's talking as calmly as he can. But the officer tells him to step back, someone will come talk to him in a little while.

In the heat and humidity of August, the afternoon sun burning down, they stand waiting. Nobody comes to talk to them. Other family members start showing up, cousins and uncles and grandparents. In a daze, one uncle crosses the yellow line to try to get a better look and the police stop him. Word starts going through the crowd: Those are the parents. People begin coming up to them and saying their son had his hands up when he was shot. A nurse tells them she heard the gunshots and ran over to help him, but the police told her to stay back. Later, it will come out that a paramedic already had declared him dead, but since nobody bothers to tell them, they're standing there thinking the cops refused medical help and just let him die.

Hysterical now, McSpadden starts screaming at the cops, the media, and even—as Brown remembers it later—at Cal. *She's not the mother. What does she need to be out here for?* Grief takes many forms, not all of them pretty. Brown pulls Cal away. His eyes stay fixed on the white sheet. The red patch around the head seems to keep spreading and spreading.

Brown is an internal person, the kind of man who takes things in and contains them until they can be tolerated. His mother is so religious she allowed only gospel music in the house. His father was a soldier who came back from Vietnam intact and worked hard and ran five miles every morning. After some rough years when he was younger—seventeen when he got McSpadden pregnant, he veered between work and street life—he started going back to church. He got a GED, drove trucks, worked construction. Now he has a steady job transporting patients in a medical van. But there's no doubt in his mind that his son has been executed, nor much doubt in the crowd around him. Everyone knows at least a few names from the long list of young Black men killed in dubious police shootings: Sean Bell, Amadou Diallou, Kimani Gray, Patrick Dorismond. Just in the last few months, police killed a man who was selling loose cigarettes on Staten Island and a young man who was looking at an air rifle in an Ohio Walmart. And many of them have been harassed as well. St. Louis is one of the most segregated cities in America, much of it the result of city policies, like its 1916 "segregation ordinance," the first such referendum in the nation. In 1917, a White riot killed more than forty-eight people, including a baby, thrown into a fire. In 1949, when Black kids were first allowed into public swimming pools, Whites rioted again. And these little Missouri towns are notorious for financing their city governments with the traffic stops of poor Black people—last year, Ferguson issued thirty-three thousand minor-crime arrest warrants for a population of twenty-one thousand, mostly for traffic violations and overwhelmingly to Black residents. (At 29 percent of the population, Whites get stopped just 12.7 percent of the time.) In the nearby town of Bel-Ridge, a traffic light was even rigged so police could change it as people entered the intersection, boosting their city budget by 16 percent. Here on Canfield, one of the roughest neighborhoods in town, the level of trust is zero.

Brown watches the cops closely, afraid they might plant a gun to justify the shooting, and sure enough, a rumor soon roils the crowd: They're saying Michael had a gun.

An hour and a half after the shooting, detectives finally arrive.

After two hours, shots go off in the distance—everyone hears them—and the police bare their weapons to the crowd, telling them to get the fuck back and calm the fuck down. They're obviously nervous, but what strikes Brown is that they turned their guns on the crowd instead of in the direction of the gunshots. *They fear us.* Then they bring out a line of police dogs to force the people back and Brown glances at his baby daughter, sitting on a little hill with his mother-in-law, and sees a police dog a few feet away from her, snapping furiously. An officer sees what's happening and tells the K-9 cops to leave the family alone, but the only bit of real kindness they remember that whole day is when the police pass out bottles of cold water among themselves and one officer—not from Ferguson— refuses because they didn't offer any to the family. He tells them what's happening isn't right but he has to do his job. *Tell your husband to get a good lawyer*, he says.

For another couple hours, the police leave the body lying in the street. Half the neighborhood is standing there without fear. A nearby TV crew calmly documents McSpadden's grief—"You took my son away from me! You know how hard it was for me to get him to stay in school and graduate? You know how many Black men graduate?"—but the trained professionals with guns and dogs are too afraid to remove the body.

Finally, the transport van pulls up, and that's when they lift the sheet for one of the cousins to see. She comes up to Brown and says it's really him. He cries out and falls to his knees.

"We spent four hours and thirty-two minutes watching him lay on the ground," Cal says later.

"On the hot ground," Brown says.

"And you could just see all the blood. Every time you looked at the sheet, it was more and more blood."

Brown looks up. "That was the most hardest thing I ever been through in life," he says in a voice that still seems stunned, so soft and distant it could be coming from inside a safe at the bottom of a river. "We was treated like we wasn't parents, you know? That's what I didn't understand. They sicced dogs on us. They wouldn't let us identify his body. They pulled guns on us."

To him, it seems like the police were trying to aggravate the crowd on purpose so they could cover up what really happened.

These days, Brown tries not to be alone. That's when pages start flipping in his mind: the day Mike was born, a little yellow bug with puffy Chinese eyes. Playing with his Tonka trucks.

Jumping in that pool they put in the backyard. Playing those video games, *Madden* and *Call of Duty*. He loved the puzzle games best, and when he beat one he'd never play it again. Sitting next to him in the car as they drove around, talking about life and women. Beaming in his cap and gown. Then the bloody sheet and the horrible thought: *I should have been there to protect him.* So in a way, it is a mercy how crazy things become. That first night, members of both sides of the family gather separately, talking about what to do. One cousin works for Ben Crump, the attorney who represented Trayvon Martin's family. Somebody makes that call. A grandfather knows Rev. Toon and gets him on the phone. Toon reaches Sharpton the next morning and Sharpton tells him to have the local office handle it. Toon says, "No, I think you need to go on the internet. This kid laid in the gutter four and a half hours." Sharpton watches the video and books a plane.

Crump is at church when his phone starts blowing up, one call after another—including a call from Tracy Martin, Trayvon's father. "Crump! They need you in St. Louis! They killed this kid and they left his body layin' in the street!" The most prominent civil-rights lawyer of his generation, Crump gets at least fifty calls like this every week. Currently, his clients include the victims of a series of "Houdini-handcuff suicide killings," in which Brown boys were handcuffed in the back of the police car and police claim they committed suicide: Victor White in Louisiana, Chavis Carter in Arkansas. Also Alesia Thomas of Los Angeles, a Black woman who died after a police officer kicked her seven times in the crotch—there's a video the court will not release for fear of another Rodney King riot. But like everyone else, he's shocked by the stark fact of the bodily desecration: that boy lying for four and a half hours in the street. He books a plane.

That morning, Brown huddles with Cal and their kids and various relatives, trying to be strong for them and doing his containment thing, packing the feelings down. He stays very quiet. He still cannot fully believe that was his son under the sheet. He's always been "mushy" with the kids, Cal says, but today it's like he's trying to hug them safe, taking comfort from the role of the protector. Later, he drops by a local radio station with Pastor Carlton Lee, a lively young preacher whose church he recently joined, still so stunned he seems to Lee "almost like a zombie." Lee tells him, "You have my support, we love you," and Brown answers, "Thank you. I need it. Pray for me." Then he goes on the radio and asks everybody to stay peaceful.

The McSpadden side of the family spends the morning at Aunt Des's house, talking obsessively about what happened. How did you find out about it? What did you hear? He had just graduated! He wasn't a bad kid! He wasn't a kid who was constantly being arrested and put in jail. He wasn't that kid! They are a family of ministers and workers. One uncle built a school in South Africa. One cousin works as a sales executive at AT&T. McSpadden worked behind a deli counter for ten years, rising to supervisor. But most of them have been hassled by police. A cousin named Eric Davis remembers the time he brought some White friends home from college, telling them to bring their college IDs because they would get pulled over—and sure enough, just as they were pulling into town, they got pulled over. His friends were astounded. Even mild-mannered Charles Ewing, a God-fearing pastor of forty years, was arrested on a mistaken charge, and the cops handcuffed him and left his sister by the side of the road. That was just one town over in Jennings, where the entire police department got disbanded a few years ago because of all the harassment.

Downtown that same morning, St. Louis County police chief Jon Belmar tells the press Brown physically assaulted the police officer who shot him. But he doesn't name the police officer, who has been placed on administrative leave with full pay.

That afternoon, the two families come together for a prayer vigil at the shooting site. A memorial of teddy bears has appeared on the fatal spot. McSpadden lays out a line of red roses and Uncle Charles says a prayer and praises all the young men and women who have gathered in peace to honor their dead brother. "The world needs to see we can come together, do it peaceably, and pray."

A police car drives past, crushing the roses. That night, the riots start.

Crump arrives the next morning. McSpadden can't stop crying. She keeps coming back to the image of her son lying in the center of the road for four and a half hours, the blood staining that white sheet as the cops cursed at them. Brown arrives soon after in a state of "great anger," as Crump remembers later. He's still trying to contain himself, but anyone can see it's eating him up inside. "They gonna try to get away with it," he says. "They gonna try to get away with it."

"You gotta fight for his legacy now," Crump tells him. "That's your fight. Nothing else."

Brown shakes his head and says nothing. He's not an activist. He just wants to see the killer punished.

Crump has been here before. He was in fourth grade when he moved to an integrated school because of someone named Thurgood Marshall and began his long climb from rural poverty to law school. He starts talking about the journey to justice, the support of civil-rights groups, the legal steps, and public campaigns. He puts Brown on the phone with Tracy Martin and Ron Davis, the father of the Georgia teenager who was shot to death for refusing to turn down his car radio. "You can't give way to emotions," he tells them. "You can't get justice by going to be unjust."

Sharpton arrives on Tuesday. Brown's still angry and locked in his underwater safe, and McSpadden still can't stop crying, but both of them are now ready to make another public call for peace. Sharpton is pleased. Some families don't know the difference between Eric Holder and Eric Clapton, but they get it—they don't want the police to be able to say *Look at what I was dealing with. I had to shoot.*

Before they leave, Sharpton has one warning for them: "They gonna go after your son. Then they coming after y'all. I've seen this playbook. Get ready for that."

Later, there will be a time to flip through that picture book. With Cal at his side, often finishing his sentences or telling a story while he nods, Brown will laugh about the swimming pool. "When he got in the pool, the pool overflowed."

"Going out to eat, just taking rides."

"Sitting around, watching a movie."

"Cooking dinner at home."

"Playing games. Barbecues."

"We would give him a mask, let him scare the kids," Brown says.

"Playing the dozens, where you just go back and forth, talking about each other."

Girlfriends? They flocked to him. He had that laid-back demeanor where you wouldn't know if he was interested. "But he had one particular girl that I feel like stole his heart," Cal says.

"She still come around," Brown says. "And she's in college."

"She has her head on straight. She's going to school for forensic science. And I can actually say that he loved her, because I remember one time they were not talking and I gave him a few little pointers. And he said, 'Cal, I love her. She gonna be my wife.'"

Brown nods, pleased. "He flirted around. But the person that he'd bring to the house, it'd be her. He didn't ever bring anybody different to the house."

Cal gets a big smile on her face. "You ain't tell him about how he was a prankster."

Brown shakes his head. "He called me . . .

"April Fool's."

"April Fool's Day. He called me and said, 'Look, I didn't want to tell you, but . . . Shae's pregnant.' And I said, 'What?'"

"No," Cal says, "You're gonna be a grandfather."

"Yeah! That's what he said. 'You're gonna be a grandfather.' And I said, 'What?' He said, 'I knew you was gonna sound like that. I'm gonna call you right back.'"

He let them stew all day. They were steamed, eight kids in the house already, saying, "How are we going to take on another kid? They both gotta go to school! We gonna have to take care of this baby!"

He finally called back around ten that night and said, "I'm just playin'. It's April Fool's." Brown hung up on him.

All that week, as the world descends on Ferguson, the two branches of the family huddle apart from each other. There's no time to mourn. The world media assembles on the sidewalks, and Brown and McSpadden hole up in separate hotels. The violence shocks them— not just the sight of police on armored vehicles aiming machine guns and lobbing tear gas at the protesters, but the shameful sight of Black men once again burning down their own streets, screaming and raging without control.

But there are fresh outrages every day: the Ferguson police refusing to wear their name badges, shooting a female preacher with a rubber bullet, roughing up reporters, handcuffing a ninety-year-old Holocaust survivor, wearing I AM DARREN WILSON wristbands, tear-gassing people standing peacefully in their own yards. When they finally release an incident report, it contains nothing but the date, time, and location. Violating both the law and their own policies, it includes no narrative of the event.

On Wednesday, Ferguson police chief Thomas Jackson tells the media that their son hit the officer in the face so hard he had to go to the hospital—another insult, like he's already building a case against their son and won't hesitate to make false claims to do it.

That night, the violence flares again—and again the militarized reaction of the Ferguson police shocks the world.

On Thursday, the governor turns the police response over to a Black Highway Patrol captain named Ron Johnson, who marches with protesters and changes the tone completely—suddenly there's music and free food. But the very next day, Jackson releases a video of Michael stealing cigarillos from a convenience store and shoving a clerk who tried to stop him—a decision denounced by the governor and opposed by the Justice Department. To the family, it feels like another desecration. Even if he did such a thing, did he deserve to be killed for it? The violence flares again.

When prosecutor Bob McCulloch refuses to allow a special prosecutor and takes the case to a grand jury, another blast of indignation rises. In Ferguson, McCulloch is infamous for defending a group of policemen who gunned down two unarmed robbery suspects at a Jack in the Box, dismissing the victims as "bums." And everyone knows his father was a policeman killed by a Black suspect. Even the St. Louis county executive called him biased. This is the impartial hand of justice?

Pastor Lee keeps bringing back reports from the protests—each time he talked the protesters into taking a couple steps back, the police took a couple steps forward. He got a call about possible vandalism at his church, and while he was driving there they pointed an M16 at his windshield and touched a gun barrel to his wife's head. He was there when they rushed the Holocaust survivor. He got shot at with rubber bullets.

He was standing next to the crew from Al Jazeera TV when the police lobbed a can of tear gas at them. They ran with their eyes burning and the Al Jazeera guy said, "I feel like I'm back in Palestine." Endlessly, they parse the crime. Dorian Johnson, the kid who was with Michael that day, said that the officer passed them and told them to "get the fuck on the sidewalk." They kept walking. He squealed his tires backing up and grabbed Michael by the throat. Dorian said that the cop's gun was already drawn and he told Michael, "I'll shoot." Michael was wearing a T-shirt, shorts, and flip-flops, nowhere to hide a gun. Why did he have to shoot him? Other witnesses tell different stories, and it's unlikely the truth of what happened will ever be certain. But there are larger truths. At his church, Brown pleads: "Pastor Lee, you know he's not a thug."

He can't think about that now. The funeral is Monday. He stays with people as much as possible, cries in his bed at night, even breaks down one night at the dinner table. He goes to church almost daily. He's doing his best to channel his anger into the long Black tradition of protest and reform. Just days after the shooting, after speaking with a local lobbyist about a law requiring that cameras be worn by all police officers, he starts wearing a T-shirt that says THE MIKE BROWN LAW. But on Sunday, he goes to a peace rally wearing a T-shirt that says NO JUSTICE, NO PEACE, which pretty well expresses the contradictions raging inside. Sitting stony-faced on a rented bus with Sharpton and Crump and various helpers and handlers, waiting to go onstage, he broods so silently—*I should have been there to protect him*—that Cal tries to nudge him. "Baby, you gotta talk." He says he doesn't know what to say, but the truth is he's still so angry he's afraid he might explode.

Finally, they usher him past flashing cameras to the stage. He looks out at the world with that thousand-yard stare, thanks them for the love and support, and asks for peace. "Will you please, please take a day of silence so I can—so we can lay our son to rest. Please. That's all I ask." They lead him back down into the flashing cameras, and the reporters rush him.

Then it's the funeral, another mob scene, 50 uncles and aunts and cousins and another 550 friends and a few thousand strangers, politicians, and celebrities, the TV cameras bristling from an elevated duck-blind across the street and camera crews stalking the crowds. Backstage, they get into a squabble about the lineup— why are so many politicians scheduled to speak? The band vamps for long stretches. Finally they file in, McSpadden touching a handkerchief to her nose, Brown numb and staring. The band breaks into a boisterous spiritual.

To Brown, it's all a blur. There are words about the Prince of Peace and what happens when the wicked advance, for we are accounted as sheep for the slaughter, and periodically the music rises and voices cry out and then an uncle named Bernard is up there in dark glasses saying that he'd be lying if he said he didn't still have anger in his heart and revenge on his mind. "But I can't be no fool. We got to do it the right way." A cousin talks about God and freedom and equality and there's more music—*he saw the best in me when everyone else around could see only the worst in me*—and more sermons and Pastor Charles talking Cain and Abel, and Cain's blood is crying from the ground just like Michael's blood is crying from the ground. Crump talks about Dred Scott, and Sharpton brings the congregation to their feet with a mixture of calls to activism and the striver's sermon heard weekly in every Black church in the land: "Blackness has never been about being a gangster or a thug. Blackness was about no matter how low we was pushed down, we rose up anyhow."

But Brown hears none of this. Too emotional to speak himself, he lets Cal speak for him. She says what she's been telling him privately, trying to stop him from blaming himself: Michael was a kind and gentle soul who was chosen by God to bring change to America. "We have had enough of seeing our brothers and sisters killed in the street," she says. "We have had enough of this senseless killing. Show up at the voting polls, let your voices be heard."

Then they file out and there's a crowd of thousands pressing against the barriers, TV cameras mobbing the hearse, the heat one hundred degrees. One woman shudders to her knees in a pouring sweat. A young man in dreadlocks gets mad because he got kicked out of the inner circle behind the barricades, where Spike Lee and other celebrities mingle with the dazed family members. He wants to know why the protesters aren't given a place of honor. "The media didn't come because of Michael's blood," he shouts. "They came because of what *we* did!"

At the cemetery, women carry umbrellas, the men sweat in their black suits. A man sings a spiritual about going home, a small choir sings "I'll Fly Away." The casket arrives in a white carriage and only then, when the box is actually being lowered into the ground, does the spell on Brown finally break. His son is dead and he can be silent no more. He cries out and throws his head back, his face a mask of unimaginable agony.

Months will pass before Brown can talk to strangers. When he tries to give an interview on CNN, he's monosyllabic.

"Did it upset you that he was left out for so long?"

"Yes."

"Is that something that still upsets you?"

"Yes."

Afterward, Cal has a talk with him. She's been sticking to hugs and prayers, but now something must be said. "You're portraying yourself as an angry Black man," she says.

"But I am angry," he answers.

"I know that you are, but if you're calling for the supporters and the protesters to be peaceful, you gotta have a better look. You can't call for peace looking like you want to hurt somebody."

The problem is he does. One of the reasons he's so fierce on the subject of peace is to remind himself.

He takes comfort from the support of the community. One of Michael's teachers even wrote a letter saying Michael was one of the kindest kids she ever taught, quiet and funny, his parents "fiercely protective" and "active in every aspect of his education." Things like that help take the sting out of the horrible glee in the right-wing media over the cigarillo video, mocking the family's "rush to judgment" about the police as they themselves rushed to judge. Maybe he was high on angel dust? Didn't he hit Officer Darren Wilson so hard he had a "blowout fracture to the eye socket"? And what about that "thug music" he made? Over and over, they linked Brown's death to the president, whom they accused of "orchestrating" the protests and dividing the country by race. Sample comment: "What holiday isn't celebrated in Ferguson? Father's Day. It's too confusing for them."

Then another terrible thing happens. The split between Brown and McSpadden was very bitter, with fights over child support and parental responsibilities, and all that history erupts when McSpadden sees Cal's mother selling Michael Brown T-shirts on West Florrisant and explodes into rage. With a group of friends and her husband, Louis Head, they swarm the T-shirt stand, taking the shirts and all the proceeds, too. Someone attacks Cal's mother's boyfriend with a pipe—exposing, in their grief and rage, the divided family's deepest troubles.

Brown starts asking Pastor Lee about the Bible. Why would God send his only begotten son to die? What was the point of that? Why would he send his son down to be a sacrifice?

A young man with an even younger face—on cold nights at the protests, he wears one of those Tibetan hats with earflaps and strings hanging down—Lee was stopped by the police so often as a teenager he would leave the house ten minutes early to accommodate. There's no doubt in his mind about the overall justice of the cause. After the killing, he even signed on as NAN's local representative. The result has been at least sixty-nine death threats from right-wing racists, including at least one that said they would burn down his church with him in it.

His answer to Brown: "What if Mike Jr. could be the equivalent of Saint Paul? What if Michael Brown Jr. is the justice martyr for us to take the injusticeness that the Black man is going through all the way around the world, to expose how people are being treated?"

Inspired, he starts writing a sermon called "Arrest Them Now": Prosecutor McCulloch decided to take the case to a grand jury rather than bring charges himself, so he's like Pontius Pilate washing his hands. The Sadducees and the Pharisees were the police chiefs who incited the people and Barabbas was Darren Wilson. When he delivers the sermon in church, Brown is sitting in the audience. "Which one do you want us to crucify? Do you want us to crucify the murderer? Or do you want us to crucify the innocent person? Kill Michael Brown and let the murderer go free?"

Brown tears up.

But when he's finally able to talk, he comes prepared to tell the sad as well as the good.

From the day Michael was born up until he was three, he was very quiet, playing by himself, not interacting with the other kids. When he was five, he started to open up. School helped at first; he loved kindergarten. But then he had a comprehension issue. He had to read a passage a couple of times over to get it. But they got tutoring and passed through that.

His size was a problem. Kids teased him, calling him fat, and one day he said he didn't want to go back to that school. "I told him, 'They're just kids that play jokes and don't know that they're hurtful jokes at that age. Why don't you laugh with them?'"

Brown's father died when Michael was eight, which hit the boy hard because they were close. He started asking questions about life then, and Brown had to tell his son that there were things you just couldn't explain.

In eighth grade, he tried out for football, but his grades suffered and Brown finally told him he had to quit. "I told him, 'Grades before sports. If you ain't got the grades, you ain't gonna be able to play no sports.'" He wasn't happy about that.

Without doubt, the turmoil in the family took its toll. When Brown and McSpadden broke up in 1999, Michael followed his mom to a new school district. Then he did a year's stint at Jennings. Sometimes he would call his father, asking to be rescued. "And the two different families, we really didn't get along, so it was kinda hard for me to go pick him up," Brown says in a pained, quiet voice.

"I had to have a family member go get him and bring him over to the house."

The first time Cal met Michael, he was about sixteen, and they came home to find him sitting on the porch. "Mike-Mike had obviously had a little spat with his mother, and then she dropped him off over there," Cal remembers. Brown was annoyed and fussing with him about being disrespectful and Michael never said a word. Finally he said, "Dad, are you finished?" Brown said he was. "Now would you like to hear my side of the story?"

Shortly after that, Michael came to stay with them. But he flat-out refused to go to school, sulking in his room for about three months. "It was a big struggle," Brown says.

"He couldn't focus," Cal says. "He didn't like it."

Brown admits he was pretty worried. "Because he kind of had his mind made up."

"He got bored," Cal says.

"Just like me," Brown says.

"He lost interest in stuff so quick."

"Just like me," Brown says.

That's when Cal stepped in. She's easygoing, a hugger, and Michael cleaved to her so eagerly that Brown got a little jealous. Michael told her things he didn't tell anyone else—that he didn't believe in God, which shocked her, and that his greatest fear was "not to be loved." With college degrees of her own, she sang the praises of knowledge. "Education is everything. Especially as a Black man. If you don't have an education, you don't have anything." He never said much in response. She'd ask him, "What do you think?" He'd say, "Well, just give me a minute."

Then Michael heard about a program where he could go to school part time and complete the credits fast. So he did that his senior year, signing a contract where he promised to keep up with the homework—and that was another struggle. When graduation came around, he turned up short on some phys-ed credits, but he buckled down for two more months—which is why he graduated at the beginning of August, just a week before he died.

They weren't thrilled with his rap songs, which had lyrics that range from "Smoking on this dope till I choke" to "I need God and my family," but Cal figured they were an outlet for venting. "Because I had told him at one time, you know, 'You can't just be angry about stuff. You have to vent.'" Brown wasn't impressed. "I listened to some of it. I basically told him, 'Just keep it as a hobby. Let's stay focused.'"

But mostly they focused on the daily happiness. He played the tuba in sixth grade, played his video games, played catch in the street, football and kickball. "Just a normal kid, man." At the thought, Brown flashes a sweet gold-toothed smile so sudden and brief it seems like a mirage.

When Cal became ill in January of 2013, Michael was her biggest supporter. If he wasn't at the hospital by her side, he was on the phone with encouraging words. When she came home, he was always there in her face. "What are you doing?" "I'm going to the mailbox." "No, you're not. Sit back down." She couldn't even carry her own purse—she laughs at the image of that huge guy tenderly carrying her purse.

That summer came something that they regarded as a sign. "You want to tell him?" Cal asks. "Or you want me to tell him?"

"You can tell him," Brown says.

"He called and he said that he had just took a picture."

"He called me," Brown says.

"It had rained, and I guess he was looking at the sunset, a tree in the right bottom corner, and then in the middle it was the moon and some clouds around it. And on the other side, it kind of looked swirly. So he sent us the picture and he was like, 'Look at it and tell me what you see.' And I said, 'I don't see nothing.' And then we started laughing."

"And he got upset," Brown says. "He was like, 'I'm serious, Dad. I'm not playing!'"

"Then my sister looked at the picture and her boyfriend, my mom—we kind of passed the phone around the house and we were like, 'We don't see it. What is it that you see?' And he said, 'In the middle, there's an angel. The devil is chasing the angel into the eyes of God.' And I told him, 'If it's truly a sign from God, it was meant for you.'"

Brown nods. "Some people see it, some people don't."

A few weeks later, he finally got to graduate. He was excited. They were all there with him and went out afterward for a celebration lunch. He seemed different, Cal says, like he was really growing up. "I took his dad back to work, and me and him hung out the entire day. We were about to move into a new home and he said, 'Am I still gonna be able to paint my room the color that I want?' And I said, 'Let's go to Lowe's and you can pick it out.'"

Three months later, that can of paint is still sitting in the back of her van.

The media loves the action in the streets, but Brown is easiest to find in churches. Today it's Greater St. Mark and there are grandmothers, grandfathers, lots of preachers from all over, local Black politicians, two choirs, and lots of earnest teenagers in Michael Brown T-shirts. Crump rallies them with a speech about the need for body cameras, the importance of voting, and forcing America to live by the Constitution. Brown sits silently, nodding to well-wishers. The next night, he's back again. "We're going to do something Michael Brown didn't get to do," Pastor Lee says, once again urging the audience to vote. A woman offers herself as a write-in for state representative. A mom talks about how hard it is to keep a kid in school. A young protester says how beautiful it was at first, protesting together instead of killing each other. A Muslim woman in full veil pleads with the young people not to burn down the community. Another man asks, "What did Billie Holiday sing?"

"Strange Fruit," someone mutters. "What is that?"

"Black men."

Brown sits silently. But the church atmosphere helps a lot, he says. "Being out in the open as of now, I don't think it's real good for me. I think I need to be in an enclosed environment. I need to keep my family safe."

The week before Thanksgiving, with the grand jury decision imminent, the governor declared a state of emergency and called in the National Guard. Brown is getting baptized for the third time. He says he's doing it to "cleanse his soul," and that he decided to do it in September, a month after his son was killed.

He arrives that Sunday morning at Lee's church—the Flood Christian Church, a former auto-repair shop built of cinder block, with low unfinished rafters, rehabbed and opened just a year ago—with Cal and all seven of their children, the baby in his arms. They're standing together, like they should be in one of those inspirational church posters with Jesus behind them and a rainbow overhead. Their teenage daughters are singers and soccer players. One even went to a soccer clinic at the White House. And it seems significant that he chose to join such a poor and intimate church—in his modesty, his humility, and his stubborn pride, he must have felt like it was the right place for him.

Lee launches into a sermon on Jephthah the Gileadite, who was denied by his father's family because his mother was a prostitute. He gets into some earthy details, confessing his own sins and imagining the things poverty might have forced some of his parishioners to do. The point is Jephthah could have taken his rejection as an indication that his life was over and he would never amount to anything, but instead he became a mighty warrior. All of this is transparently aimed at Brown. "How many of you have lost more than you can imagine this year alone?" he asks.

Brown raises his hand.

"You must understand that in the breaking season, there has to be a restoration that immediately follows," Lee says. "God would never break you without restoring you to a better place."

They pray in a circle, holding hands.

Afterward, as they prepare to caravan over to a church that has a baptismal pool—the Flood is too poor to have its own—Brown talks about his plans for Christmas. He's going to dress up as Santa Claus and give away gifts. Yesterday, he and Cal gave out ninety Thanksgiving turkeys door to door. They're doing their best to "turn a negative into a positive," he says.

As he speaks, Brown keeps one eye firmly on his toddler, breaking off to mind him. "Where's your jacket? Put on your jacket." Half an hour later, Pastor Lee climbs into the baptismal pool. "Hit me with that old-school song," he says, and unaccompanied voices sing, "Take me to the water, take me to the water, take me to the water to be baptized." Cal goes first and comes out to applause. Then it's Brown's turn. He takes the hands of Lee and a deacon and steps gingerly into the tub, another rare smile on his face. "In obedience to the great head of the church," Lee intones, "we baptize this young man upon the confession of his faith in Christ." Then he takes one of Brown's arms as a deacon holds the other and dunks him backward into the tub—"None but the righteous, none but the righteous"—hauling up him again to cheers and hallelujahs. Brown comes up grinning. Cal hands him a towel and hugs him.

For a moment, he says, he wasn't thinking about anything.

The next morning, the day when the grand jury will complete its work and the prosecutor will announce the decision in prime time, Cal sits down at the Flood for a private talk. When she heard about the cigarillo video, she says, she couldn't believe it because it really, really, really did seem out of character. Everyone who knew him felt that way. But then her kids came home and said, "Momma, we saw the video and . . . it's Mike-Mike."

When she finally saw it for herself, it ripped through her. "I've never seen him like that. I knew that he was angry, but I thought that we had kind of got, you know, through that."

She remembers a fight he got into earlier in the year. The way he told the story, some guys on Canfield jumped him because his size made him a challenge. "He was so upset. He was like, 'I didn't even do anything, Cal.' "

For a few minutes, she diverts herself with happier stories, the way her kids jumped on him when he came in the door, his glee when she bought big glass plates to fit his jumbo-sized meals. Sometimes he'd call her just to hang out, or beg her to bring Chinese to school for lunch. "I think his past tore him apart," she says. "You know, because for a long time he didn't feel like he had a purpose."

She told him he was going to be a great father because the kids loved him so much. And she would hug him and he would hold her so tight. "Nobody has ever hugged me as much as you," he said once. She really thought he had turned the corner. On Sundays, when she and her mother would have a fellowship, he would usually sit there listening to his music. But lately, he started leaving one earphone off. Then he started taking his earphones off altogether. "He would be asking questions about the things we did as a family, how we fellowship. He would catch me reading my Bible and he would be like, 'What are you reading?' So then it just got to the point where, on Sunday mornings when he heard us, he would just automatically get up because he knew we were goin' in the kitchen to play our music and laugh and talk and cook. It was like the music opened his eyes. You know, because I would see his foot patting, like 'I'mma do it, but I'm not gonna let nobody know I'm doin' it.'"

One day, they went for a picnic and they were lying on the blankets looking up at the sky. She said, "Dude, you say you don't believe in God. Just look around! How do you think this happened?" He asked her, "So how did it begin?" She told him to read Genesis and Revelation and bought him a Bible, but he would read it only with her. "If he was at one of his grandmothers' houses, he would call me. 'You sleepin'?' 'No, I'm not sleeping.' He'd say, 'You wanna read together?'"

At this point Brown, who has been doing a local TV interview in another room, comes into the church. Cal asks what questions he got.

"Do I forgive Darren Wilson."

"Babe, you were supposed to say yes."

"I did."

"Do you?"

"No."

Cal laughs and Brown clarifies. "His actions, what he chose. Might actually be a good guy, just had a bad day."

That night, as their town burns, Brown stays at a hotel with Cal, once again trying to contain himself. The denial of a jury trial is devastating to him, the violence that follows also devastating. The next morning, he shows up for a press conference at the Greater St. Mark Family Church with red eyes above dark shadows, staring stonily as his lawyers denounce the prosecutor, Bob McCulloch. He was more like a defense attorney than a prosecutor, they say. He dismissed the witnesses whose testimony was detrimental to Wilson and endorsed the ones who were exculpatory. Twelve witnesses report that Michael had his hands up, only two say he did not. Guess which witnesses McCulloch seemed to believe? He let Wilson talk for four hours without any cross-examination. Later, it comes out that McCulloch's team also gave the grand jury instructions on the use of force based on a law that had been overturned by the Supreme Court in 1985, telling them the instructions were outdated only at the last minute and without explaining the current, more restrictive law. As they talk, Brown nods a few times. At one point, he lowers his head and hides his face under his hat brim. When he lifts his head again, his face looks exhausted and stoic and agonized, like a man determined not to cry out under torture.

Two days later, Mike Brown gives thanks. Down in the man cave, the call comes from up the stairs. Time to eat! The family gathers around the Thanksgiving table, standing because there's too much food and too many people to sit down. Oscar Grant's uncle takes his picture of the family sitting somberly with the empty chair. They bow their heads as Toon gives the blessing, talking of God and their loss and the long arc of justice. Cal's mother explains the family's unique traditions. Every year, they write their names and something they're grateful for on the tablecloth in indelible ink, then wash it and save it with all the other Thanksgiving tablecloths going back years. And the chairs are wrapped in white ribbon to honor family members who have passed on—Mike's father, Lubie; uncles and aunts; and now Mike-Mike. Brown drapes one of his T-shirts over the back of the chair, keeping an eye on the toddlers underfoot.

Dig in! Ham hocks and green beans, turkey, ribs, mac and cheese, dressing, corn, and did you get any of the oxtail and beans? An uncle grows them himself, in his yard, they're organic. And don't worry about being so polite—grab that food while it's still there.

Ready for dessert? Cal's mother spoons some banana pudding into a plastic to-go cup, and man is it sweet. On the tablecloth, people have written thanks for God, for family, for being with good people, for Mike-Mike. Cal wrote "family and favor," meaning God's favor and all his small blessings. Brown hasn't written anything.

Back in the man cave, the men talk about the game, absent relatives, the old homestead down in Mississippi, and those damn coyotes that keep going after the chickens. Brown laughs and leans back into the sofa, smoking another Newport as the men drift into an extended conversation of different stadiums and games they've seen—Edward Jones Dome has gotten so bad it's worse than a teen club, one says, and Brown laughs loud at the slam. The sound is startling after all his shy smiles. He saw the Redskins in Washington and made the mistake of wearing his Rams hat. "Them fans are pissed off—they were upset. They were about to riot outside."

No one bothers to mention how differently such a riot would be received. That knowledge is implicit, bred in their bones, a fact of American life, like crappy schools and dead-end jobs and highway stops and the old friends who died from gunfire. Then, without prompting, Brown gets closer than ever to facing that cigarillo video. "I don't know about his actions. But I know his heart. I know my son." As to what happened at the police car, if the cop grabbed him, Mike-Mike might have tried to pull his arm away. "He was a teenager," he says.

In the morning, he has to fly to Miami for yet another event. Even if he were capable of pushing these things out of his mind, history and his own new sense of responsibility require him to do otherwise.

Cal comes down. "Do you realize we have to get up in a few hours?" she says. Brown just gives her a squeeze and turns back to the game. He can be tired tomorrow. He'll put in his earbuds on the plane and when they get there, he'll walk down the Jetway and try to be the person history has summoned. But please let this moment last a little bit longer.

He walks a guest to the door, accepts words of gratitude.

"Aww, you gonna tear up?" he says, smiling warmly. "Keep in touch," he says. He stands out in the night air, taking in a moment away from his holiday gathering.

Tonight, everyone wrote on the tablecloth except for Brown. But what would he write? What can he possibly be thankful for at a time like this?

He thinks for a moment. Some answers in this world are easy—for Cal, obviously. His mother-in-law, who made her. And being able to get up every morning to fight for Mike-Mike.

The other answers are all in the future, in the ideal America that never quite comes, in the endless struggle that will deliver us—as it is delivering Brown—to grace.

THE

ABORTION

MINISTRY

OF

DR. WILLIE

PARKER

In 2014, the Pink House is the last clinic in Mississippi where a woman can get an abortion, and the state is trying to shut it down—a goal finally achieved when Mississippi banned almost all abortions in 2022. Meet the abortion doctor who is also a Christian raised in the South. He's on a mission from his own personal God.

PERFECTLY BALD, with a salt-and-pepper goatee, a small gold hoop gleaming in his left ear, and a warm smile on his dark brown face, Dr. Willie Parker enters the waiting room. Eleven young women and one tired forty-three-year-old mother sit in a circle of chairs, regarding him with somber expressions. Eight are Black. Four are White. One has jittery legs that never stop moving. Another has giant false eyelashes in constant motion. The rest are absolutely still, sitting with straight backs, like good students or condemned prisoners. One has her hair in a tight bun, another wears a Nefertiti head wrap, another wears a baseball hat that says LOVE and a T-shirt that says SOUTHERN GIRLS KNOW HOW TO PINCH A TAIL. Some have freckles, some wear glasses. One looks like a Botticelli painting, with skin so luminous it seems to shimmer. They are nurses and college students, clerks and saleswomen. One is in high school. One dances in a strip club. Another just got out of the army.

"Good morning," Parker begins, launching into a spiel he will repeat four times that day, "I am one of two doctors who travel to Mississippi to provide abortion care."

This is because no doctor in Mississippi is willing to provide such a service. Although the state already has some of the most restrictive abortion laws in the country, including a twenty-four-hour waiting period, parental consent, face-to-face counseling with the physician, and a ban on the use of Medicaid funding (except in extraordinary cases), it is going all out to close this clinic, the last abortion provider in Mississippi, known as the Pink House because the defiant woman who owns it painted it pink to make it stand out, bold and unashamed. The latest fight is over whether abortion doctors should be required to have admitting privileges at a nearby hospital in the event of a complication, an irrelevant requirement since a hospital's emergency-room staff usually does the admitting. It's a practice no other specialty is required to observe. The American Congress of Obstetricians and Gynecologists opposes the state law that makes this a requirement. But a similar law may soon leave the state of Texas—home to twenty-seven million people—with just six abortion clinics. It is already law in North Dakota, Tennessee, Texas, and Utah and looms over Alabama, Kansas, Pennsylvania, Wisconsin, Oklahoma, and Louisiana and is likely to spread to other states, pressed by a nationwide conservative movement that uses regulation to force a result democratic votes cannot achieve. So Parker flies down from his home in Chicago for several days twice a month to perform the service so few other doctors are willing to provide.

"As you know," he continues, "there's been a lot of press recently about the efforts that the state is making to close this clinic. And we're fighting that. Just Monday, we were in New Orleans at the federal-court hearing. Right now we are waiting for them to rule on the changes in the law that would make us close. It might be a few weeks, might be a few months. But the bottom line is today the clinic is still open, so we can provide care for you. And that's what we're going to do."

Many of these women come from hours away, one from a little town on the Kentucky border that's a seven-hour drive. They don't know much about Dr. Parker. They don't know that he grew up a few hours away in Birmingham, the second youngest son of a single mother who raised six children on food stamps and welfare, so poor that he taught himself to read by a kerosene lamp and went to the bathroom in an outhouse; that he was born again in his teenage years and did a stint as a boy preacher in Baptist churches; that he became the first Black student-body president of a mostly White high school, went on to Harvard and a distinguished career as a college professor and obstetrician who delivered thousands of babies and refused to do abortions. They certainly don't know about the "come to Jesus" moment, as he pointedly describes it, when he decided to give up his fancy career to become an abortion provider. Or that, at fifty-one, having resigned a prestigious job as medical director of Planned Parenthood, he's preparing to move back south and take over a circuit roughly similar—for safety reasons, he won't be more specific—to the one traveled by Dr. David Gunn before an antiabortion fanatic assassinated him in 1993. Or that his name and home address have been published by an antiabortion Web site with the unmistakable intent of terrorizing doctors like him. Or that he receives threats that say, "You've been warned." Or that he refuses to wear a bulletproof vest, because he doesn't want to live in fear—"if I'm that anxious, they've already taken my life"—but owns a stun gun because a practical man has to take precautions. What they do know is this:

He is the doctor who is going to stop them from being pregnant.

Today Parker is wearing green medical scrubs, and tomorrow he'll be wearing an orange T-shirt that says VOTING IS SEXY. His authority is in his manner, warm but always scientific. "There's some things that the state requires me to tell you," he begins. "Some of the information I'm required to give you is designed to discourage you or to scare you about the decision you're making, so I'm going to tell you the things that I have to tell you by law, but I'm also going to tell you what in my best medical opinion is more important for you to know."

In an almost priestly cadence, he builds a sermon around the word *required*. The first thing he's required by state law to explain is the possibility of complications. He could poke a hole in a uterus. There could be a life-threatening hemorrhage or infection, or damage to the bowel, fallopian tubes, ovaries, or bladder. There's also a possibility that their womb could be so severely injured a hysterectomy would be required, which would mean they couldn't have babies in the future.

With this news, the faces of the women become even more somber. The still ones remain completely still; the jittery ones get more jittery.

"But guess what?" he continues with another reassuring smile. "Those are all the exact same risks that go with having a baby. In fact, they're more likely to happen giving birth than they are with an abortion; a woman is ten times more likely to die in childbirth than she is having an abortion."

The women's faces show relief. Some of the motionless ones finally shift position.

"The second thing that I'm required to tell you is that if the reason you are having an abortion is financial, then the person you are pregnant by could be required to provide you with financial assistance."

One of the women laughs.

"The third thing is that the state requires us to give this brochure," he says, pointing to a stack of pamphlets. "It has information about adoption and other things that you might find useful. We're required to offer it to you, but you don't have to take it."

Nobody reaches for the brochure.

"And the final thing I'm required to tell you is the thing that I object to the most as a scientist and as a doctor. I'm required by law to tell you that having an abortion increases your risk for breast cancer. There is no scientific or medical evidence that supports that. The people against abortion outside yell that at women all the time. But the overwhelming majority of the studies show that that's not the case. Abortions actually protect your health."

With that, Parker finally moves on to the medical details they really want to hear. They will be given antibiotics and pain medicine, the women who are less than nine weeks can choose to have surgery or take abortifacient pills, which now account for 23 percent of American abortions. The pluses and minuses are a small pinch versus heavy bleeding, instant results versus a return visit in two weeks. But the decision is up to them. "I've never had one," he says.

As a group, the women laugh.

Now it's time for questions. One woman asks if the large cysts in her womb will be a problem. Another asks if she has to go to a pharmacy for the abortion pills. Another complains that her doctor refused to treat her vaginal infection because the drugs could cause a birth defect, even though she told him she was planning to end the pregnancy. Another asks how long they'll have to wait. Parker answers all their questions in generous detail, explaining the science and making jokes wherever he can. The relief the women feel is visible in their bodies. The jittering slows. The rigid postures relax.

"The last thing I want to say is a lot of times when you come, there might be protesters. There are people that are going to be telling you that what you're doing is wrong. It's immoral. That you can't be a Christian. That you're going to hell. And a lot of women that bothers. Because there are women here who also have religious belief, who also feel like they're Christians."

A Black woman nods.

"I see women who are crying because they are Christians," he continues, "and they are torn up by the fact that they don't believe in abortion but they're about to have one. What I tell them is that doesn't make you a hypocrite. You can never say what you will do until you're in the situation, and Christians get in jacked-up situations, too."

The woman nods again, twice.

"And I address this because if those people are getting inside your head and you're feeling conflicted, if you are not comfortable with what you're doing, you may be processing this far longer than you need to. There's nothing immoral about taking care of your health. There's nothing immoral about making the decision to not become a parent before you want to become one. There's more than one way to understand religion and spirituality and God. I do have belief in God. That's why I do this work. My belief in God tells me that the most important thing you can do for another human being is help them in their time of need."

At this, the women exchange glances.

Parker continues, spending more time on this issue than on anything else. One in three women will have an abortion by the time she's forty-five, he tells them. "Y'all talk about your shoes, you talk about where you work, where you bought your dress, but y'all ain't going to say, 'Oh girl, when did you have your abortion?' So I'm saying that if you are sitting in a room full of women, the only person you can really be sure about having an abortion is you. And you got to be comfortable with you."

So this is between you and your conscience, he tells them. "If you are comfortable with your decision, ignore everything from everybody else."

By this time, something unexpected has happened. This disparate group of a dozen women, who walked into this room not knowing who they would meet or what they would find, having only crisis in common, has become united, a team. A slender young White woman wearing Dickies work pants—the one who was recently in the army—speaks up as if she's speaking for all of them: "Doing this as a group helps us to see that we are not the only ones. Being able to speak to each other about a decision we are about to make, even if it's not close friends and family, it's very helpful."

"I'm happy to hear that," Parker says. "Because part of the suffering is when people feel like they are on their own. And that's why we have to keep it safe and legal."

In fact, the army veteran adds, she'd like to get involved with the clinic—to contribute somehow.

Parker beams and tells her to talk to him later.

He's ready to stop now—in the next step he will be doing private consultations with each of them—but the women don't want to let him go. What birth control should they take? Are the abortion pills or surgery more likely to preserve their ability to have babies in the future? Can they follow up with their regular doctors, or will they refuse even that? He answers all their questions and moves on to another room and another group of women, giving the same speech almost word for word.

This time, during the question session, a young White woman asks what happens in surgery when you're fourteen weeks pregnant. She has hair the color of straw, and she's wearing a college sweatshirt.

Parker starts to give a technical answer but stops when the woman starts to cry. "Is your concern also what it means for the fetus?" he asks.

She wipes away her tears. "I'm in a bad situation and I just can't have the baby right now—it's just a bad time."

Parker tries to soothe her, but this makes her weeping only more intense. She's scared, she says. "And I don't want to take any risks that could cause other people to know about it."

Parker nods and continues in a softer voice: "I can tell you that in the last four years, we have not transferred one patient to the hospital. The likelihood of being transferred to the hospital after an abortion is 0.3 percent."

Her tears slow down as he continues at length, applying a treatment method he calls "verbicaine." She's in college trying to get a degree, she got dumped by her boyfriend, her parents are very conservative, her hometown is the tiny place near the Kentucky border, seven hours away. But she didn't want to do this anywhere near there.

"Well, that just kind of shows what the reality is for women in this state," Parker says to her. "We've got one clinic and they're trying to close it."

When Parker was ten, his mother moved from the house with no electricity and plumbing into his grandfather's place. To get to that neighborhood, you drive past a gravel plant. Here, the world is coated with gray dust. Parker's youngest brother points out the sights: "They call that the lie tree, because everybody set up under that tree and drink and tell lies."

Their grandfather's house is simple, square, made of weathered boards that were never painted. The house that didn't have plumbing is a few streets over, abandoned now, a lone shoe left behind on the porch.

One street over is an area they called the "White Quarter." Its backyards adjoined the Parker yard, but the Blacks were never supposed to cross the line, much less drive down the White street. Naturally, the boys took this as a challenge. "It was a thrill to get on your bike and go down that hill. Three or four of us would get at the top and yell Go! And we just shoot down the road. Next thing you know, the dogs all come out running at you—or somebody shoot at you."

When he went off to college, Parker was still wearing a Jesus pin in his lapel every day and devoted his Saturday mornings to knocking on dorm-room doors to spread the Word. But that was the fall of 1981, when Reagan was funding the contras in Nicaragua and apartheid in South Africa was making the news, and his professors threw out one moral challenge after another. "Now it's not just about Jesus gets you to heaven and you live fine with pie in the sky by and by but what is your role as a Christian in the modern world?"

One professor even asked him to write a paper on abortion. His answer was rooted in "Thou shalt not kill," but he was already reluctant to judge. "My hope was that women would approach the question prayerfully," he remembers.

After medical school, he bought a big house and a nice car and overstuffed his refrigerator the way people from poverty do, but those satisfactions soon seemed empty. He dated but never quite settled down. Inspired by Gandhi's idea that the Gospel should appear to a hungry man in the form of bread, he went to work in a food pantry. But gradually, the steady stream of women with reproductive issues in his practice focused his mind. He thought about his mother and sisters and the grandmother who died in childbirth and began to read widely in the literature of civil rights and feminism. Eventually he came across the concept of "reproductive justice," developed by Black feminists who argued that the best way to raise women out of poverty is to give them control of their reproductive decisions. Finally, he had his "come to Jesus" moment and the bell rang. This would be his civil-rights struggle. He would serve women in their darkest moment of need. "The protesters say they're opposed to abortion because they're Christian," Parker says. "It's hard for them to accept that I *do* abortions because I'm a Christian." He gave up obstetrics to become a full-time abortionist on the day, five years ago, that George Tiller was murdered in church.

Now he rushes around all the time, flying from Chicago to Philadelphia to Birmingham, where he picks up a car at his brother's house and drives to the pink building in the artsy district of Jackson, where he proceeds down a hall lined with women waiting on plastic chairs to the saddest little desk you've ever seen—actually part of a hutch ripped from its base and turned to the middle of the room, raw wallboard showing. The women now come in one by one, asking questions they didn't want to ask in the group.

"Can I call and change my mind?"

"Can I go back to work the next day?"

"Can my mom be in the room with me?"

The oldest woman of the group says she has a son who's nineteen and a daughter who's seventeen, and she just had a baby two years ago who died of a heart defect. "She came home and everything," she says in a mournful voice. Plus she's anemic but not taking drugs for it. And she has asthma. And possibly a touch of bronchitis.

Another woman asks how long it will take before she can wear tampons again. "I know this sounds so selfish and everything, but I'm going to the beach next week—don't think I'm a selfish person!"

Several women say they've always been against abortion, but they're not emotionally or financially ready to have a baby. "I just wish that people that are so against it could understand," one says. "These old men out here protesting do not have vaginas or uteruses."

"Preach," Parker says.

"It just makes me so mad!"

Parker's beaming again, grinning wide. If this happened to men, he says, abortion would be free and they'd pass out free Super Bowl tickets and have public ceremonies to celebrate our brothers who went through the tough decision. He wishes more women had her righteous indignation instead of shame.

When the skinny army veteran comes in, Parker tells her she made his day with her offer to contribute. Most women are just relieved to get it over with. They never want to see this place again.

"Actually, I want to apply for a job," she says.

"You should," he says.

"I will," she replies. "Even if I don't get a job, I'll still come back and volunteer. I just want to be a part of this."

The next woman, the one with the giant eyelashes, is worried about how taking the abortion pills will affect her work. "I dance," she says.

"You can dance."

"Not with a pad on."

Another woman is already sixteen weeks, and he tells her she has to come tomorrow or she'll be too far.

"Too far for what?"

"To have an abortion in Mississippi."

"Really?"

"Really. Your last day to have an abortion in Mississippi will be Monday, and we're not going to be open on Monday."

"So I have to come tomorrow?" She repeats it as if she can't believe it. "Next week I'll be too far? I have to come tomorrow?"

Correct, he says.

She takes out her cell phone and presses the buttons. When someone answers, she tells him next week will be too late. She listens for a moment, then interrupts. "You not getting it—by Monday it will be too late for me to have an abortion in Mississippi period. You got the money?"

Finally, the sad college student comes in. They talk for a while about her tiny hometown, where she goes to college, an impending visit from her parents. After they discuss her concerns about cramping and bleeding and whether it will be so bad her parents will notice, Parker asks what she's studying.

"Forensic science," she says.

What exactly? he asks.

"Fingerprint analysis, DNA analysis, and stuff like that. They make you take chemistry and biology and stuff like that."

He teases her about getting on one of those *CSI* shows and finally gets a laugh out of her.

In all these interactions, even if it has nothing to do with abortion, Parker never misses a chance to offer comfort. This seems to be his version of absolution, often delivered with a moral. There's no reason to be ashamed of being a dancer, he tells the dancer. "That's how you make your living." And asking about tampons and the beach is not a selfish question. "Part of the reason women feel judged is they're made to feel selfish." And yes, if you must, you can probably go to work the next day. "Black women used to give birth to babies and keep picking cotton, you know, so maybe it's in your legacy to be strong."

Each time, he asks when they want to get it done.

"Tomorrow."

"Tomorrow."

"As soon as possible."

When one woman leaves, she thanks him three times. "Thank you, thank you, thank you."

He tells her to take care.

After she leaves, he takes a moment. "Sometimes women have that look in their eyes—*Whatever you do, don't say no to me.* That's . . . you know . . . I think that's too much power for anybody to have over somebody's life."

On that day, the women come, one after another after another. Parker is down here only twice a month, and as the need is great, the cases get backed up, forcing him sometimes to see as many as forty-five women in a single day. A Cajun from New Orleans says she's got finals next week, she's studying health science on scholarship, was thinking of going to nursing school. She also runs track.

"What is your event?" he asks.

"I do the 200, the 4x100, 4x400—do it all."

"Did you qualify for nationals?"

"No," she says.

"Maybe next year," he says.

The next woman is in school, too, and she already has one daughter.

The next woman is eight weeks and two days. She has to work tomorrow. "Can I go to work?"

The next woman is six weeks and one day, and she's in school, too. "I want to be a physical therapist. I plan to go to the university medical school."

He says he'll take care of her.

The next woman wants to know if she'll see anything.

"Right now there's not a whole lot there," he assures her.

"That little sac is about the size of my pinkie now. It's not like the pictures of the baby parts that the antiabortion people show you."

She wants him to know she's opposed to abortion, at least in principle. "I don't believe in it. If I caught it later and it was just like a whole little person . . . but I know I can't be the parent I want to be for my child."

Another patient is in high school, a sweet-looking blond. She comes in with her mother. Parker asks the mother to step out for a moment. When she's gone, he tells the daughter that sometimes the parent is the one who is pushing the idea. "Is this your idea to have an abortion? Do you feel comfortable with your decision?"

She says she's fine with it.

The next woman, the forty-three-year-old, already has two kids, plus she's recovering from thyroid cancer. "Actually, I want my tubes tied." she tells him. "I really don't want any more kids."

"I hear you," he says.

She works at a religious hospital, she adds. "They don't know I'm doing this. That's why I want to do the pill. I just want to make it seem like I had a miscarriage."

In an ideal world, he tells her, her doctor could have done her abortion and fixed her tubes at the same time so she wouldn't have to go through the risk of two procedures. "But in Mississippi," he says, "you're getting the best you can get."

Another woman comes, and then another and another—and this one, slender and very beautiful, says it's impossible she's six weeks pregnant because she hasn't had sex but one time, four weeks ago.

"I don't know what to tell you, my sister," he says with a laugh. "All I can tell you is that there's something in your uterus."

"We gotta get it out of there," she says.

He can help with that, he assures her.

"I'm just going to go lesbian," she says.

"I've done abortions on three lesbians," he tells her.

She gasps. "Lesbians fucking?"

"Yeah, they do. Every now and then someone falls off the wagon."

"I'm, like, in total dismay," she says.

"How you get down is nobody's business," he tells her, "but you don't have to switch your diet up like that."

She laughs. "Look at you defending me."

"That's part of the issue. People don't think women are supposed to enjoy sex. So when you enjoy sex—"

"It's like, 'Oh, you whore!'"

"Owning your sexuality and making good choices about it— that's the thing I endorse. Run it; don't let it run you."

She nods. "Okay, I feel better."

The next woman is fifteen weeks and two days and can't take time off from work this week. He tells her that if she doesn't come tomorrow, she won't be able to have an abortion in Mississippi.

She gasps. "Oh no!"

"You are going to slip and break your leg just for a day," he says. "And we'll give you a note that won't say abortion clinic on it."

Another woman comes in. Her question is simple: "How much is it?"

When the consultations are over, Parker vents. These poor women have to come through all those verbal assaults from the "Antis," as he calls them, the taunting and the judgment and the cloying malice of their prayers. But the Antis never ask the hardest question: If they really think abortion is murder, how long should a woman be in prison? Instead, they go after the doctors. And other doctors will say, Bless you, you're so brave, but they turn women away and often don't even refer them to someone who will help them. And some will say smugly, We don't do that here, failing to recognize that what he does allows them to make that smug declaration, allows them to present themselves as noble caregivers while they send their most desperate patients out to fend for themselves.

And don't get him started on the state's fight for admitting privileges. The Pink House does about two thousand abortions a year, and CDC records say that Mississippi residents get six thousand abortions a year. The state used this as evidence that women could always go outside the state, making it fine to shut down the Pink House—the exact same argument, as it happens, that segregationists once used to keep Mississippi colleges White. But the reality is women with money will do what they did pre-*Roe*: Their expensive private doctors will counsel them on exactly the right words to use about mental trauma and suicidal tendencies so that the hospital board will rule the termination of their pregnancy a medical necessity. But the women who come to this clinic are often poor women of color who can't afford to go outside the state and who can't afford the expensive consultations on just the right words to say. "They're the ones who have to do the perp walk," Parker says. The Antis, who call themselves pro-life, don't seem to care that before *Roe v. Wade*, hundreds of women a year died trying to terminate their own pregnancy or from an illegal abortion, a disproportionate number of them minorities. "We know what happens when abortion is illegal," Parker says. "Women suffer and they die. But when abortion is safe and legal, patient mortality goes virtually to zero."

And now the famously conservative Fifth Circuit court, the same court that upheld a similar restrictive law in Texas, has the fate of these women in its hands. The federal district court overruled Mississippi on the basis that the law would leave the state without a single abortion clinic. But Governor Phil Bryant, who has promised to make Mississippi "an abortion-free zone," is confident that the appellate court will see things his way. After all, he has said that he is now simply trying to protect women's health. But women haven't been showing up in the emergency room with injuries or complications, he says. There's never been a report from the Mississippi Department of Health suggesting that complications from abortion are high. The law seeks to solve a problem that does not exist, and its regulations are completely arbitrary, an abuse of regulatory authority. And it all comes back to the early Judeo-Christian narratives that say the fall of man was caused by a woman, Parker says. "That's woven into our culture, and it has to be deconstructed at every level."

One result: In 2012, America's teenage girls had an average of thirty-one births per one thousand. In Canada, the number was fourteen. In France, six. In Sweden, seven. The difference is that those countries promote contraception without shame. "So it seems like if they want to reduce abortion, the best thing to do would be to support contraception—but they're against contraception, too, because contraception and abortion decouple sexuality from procreation. That's why I think religious preoccupation with abortion is largely about controlling the sexuality of women."

But what bothers him the most, he continues, is the argument that abortion is a secret plot to kill Black babies. At a time when African Americans are suffering tremendous amounts of economic disparity and human suffering, the Antis want to compound the suffering by making people feel conflicted about controlling the size of their families—like that nursing student this morning who had to juggle her abortion with her finals next week. "The people who talk about Black genocide are the same people who defund Head Start and food stamps and are now trying to dismantle public education by encouraging voucher systems—all of the systems that need to be in place to take care of those Black babies. It's diabolical."

A clinic aide interrupts. Two more groups of women are ready for the orientation.

The next day, Parker does abortions. By the entrance to the parking lot, beside walls decorated with defiant signs that say JESUS DIDN'T SHAME WOMEN, PRAY TO END SIDEWALK BULLYING, JUDGE NOT LEST YOU BE JUDGED, and DR. PARKER IS A HERO, two patient escorts stand beside a portable boom box playing defiant songs, like Tom Petty's "I Won't Back Down." Across the driveway stand four protesters with signs about murder and dead babies. At the sight of an unfamiliar face, one of them takes out a camera and snaps a picture.

When the high school girl and her mom arrive, one of the escorts tells them to park down the hill and she'll walk them back up, steering them past the protesters.

The escort's name is Michelle Colon. She's been doing this for ten years, and she has her own abortion story about herbs from an elder and the emergency room. Things are quiet today because there's a lull while they wait for the Fifth Circuit's decision, but she's seen fifty protesters out here screaming at women as they enter or emerge from the clinic. Sometimes they surround a car and shove their pamphlets through the window, shouting "Mommy, don't kill me." To patients of color, they say, "You're going to kill the next

Obama, you're going to kill the next Martin Luther King." They call Colon the "deathscort."

On the patio nearby, the high school girl's mother waits. She doesn't want to give her name, because she doesn't want her husband to know they're here. "He would just be shitty about it," she says. "He comes from one of those really strict Catholic backgrounds."

Sitting under the awning, they gripe about Mississippi. Although it has the highest obesity rate, the highest rate of gonorrhea, the highest child-mortality rate, and one of the highest teenage-pregnancy rates, the governor turned down Obamacare's Medicaid expansion. But they're number one in religion.

While they talk, women come out of the clinic one by one. Some breeze out, some look shaken. One clutches her belly. Now it's the former soldier coming out, head held high and shoulders back. She's a nurse, twenty-five. She says the protesters were very intimidating when she came in and that helped spark her desire to work here. "I'm a Christian. I go to church every Sunday. I believe Jesus Christ is the one true savior of the world. But the way they're going about this is not going to bring people to Christ. They're not doing it with dignity and respect and compassion."

And what brought her here?

As she answers, her voice begins to shake: "Um, my husband passed away—he committed suicide. He committed suicide in front of his family. I already have one son with him, and I just feel very alone. I don't have the means—the financial means—to raise another child."

She presses on, fighting back tears. "Also, right now my mental state is not . . . appropriate for a young child. So I would like to address my mental health and seek out therapy and counseling before I bring another life into this world."

Behind her, the escorts are wiping away tears, and the protesters shout their imprecations. Colon goes to the boom box and cranks it up:

In a world that keeps on pushing me around,
but I'll stand my ground.

That night Dr. Parker drives his old Volkswagen to Montgomery, Alabama. He's due at the clinic there at 6:15 in the morning.

Driving in the dark, Parker gets reflective. He remembers leaving for college thirty years ago, when he didn't want to stop in Mississippi because the state's ugly racial history made the trees seem taller and the skies seem darker. Now we're driving the Freedom Trail in reverse, heading toward the turnout where the bus got firebombed and the spot where a lone white protest marcher was shot dead and Black protesters picked up his sign and continued on. In an hour or two, we'll get to Selma and the famous bridge where the Alabama police launched their savage attack on civil-rights marchers.

Parker's mind spins back to childhood. His mother was a very kind woman but a disciplinarian from the old school—if somebody took your bike, she'd send you to get it back. She had her first baby at seventeen and died at fifty-three, worn out by six children and a life of manual labor, but she was trying to get her GED when she died and she took them to the Faith Chapel Christian Center three days a week. They never knew they were poor. "We had penny candy, we played hopscotch, we had all these simple pleasures."

Being bullied had an impact, definitely. He remembers what it's like to be terrorized. That fueled the search for social justice that led him, eventually, to theologians like Paul Tillich, Dr. King, and Dietrich Bonhoeffer, the Lutheran pastor who wrestled with "Thou shalt not kill" before joining a plot to assassinate Adolf Hitler. "He said the kind of Christianity that does not radicalize you with regard to human suffering is inauthentic— cheap and easy grace."

His "come to Jesus" moment occurred in Hawaii. He was teaching at the university when a fundamentalist administrator began trying to ban abortions in the school clinic, throwing students with an unwanted pregnancy into a panic. One day, he was listening to a sermon by Dr. King on the theme of what made the Good Samaritan good. A member of his own community passed the injured traveler by, King said, because they asked, "What would happen to me if I stopped to help this guy?" The Good Samaritan was good because he reversed the question: "What would happen to this guy if I don't stop to help him?" So Parker looked in his soul and asked himself, "What happens to these women when abortion is not available?"

He knew the answer.

At midnight, he arrives at a modest hotel called the SpringHill Suites—with five hours to sleep before he rises for his next shift.

At the Mongomery clinic, one of the last three abortion clinics in Alabama, Parker gives a quick tour of things that violate his sense of justice. At the cost of $40,000, the state required the owner to move the air conditioners into a fireproof closet with reinforced doors in addition to adding new alarms and lights—all completely unnecessary. "They don't have anything to do with safety. It's about consumption of your resources." He chats with the clinic owner, a woman named June Ayres, who hobbles badly from bone cancer but, after thirty-six years at the clinic, won't give up working all day, every day, trading stories about the many forms of harassment they've experienced—the plastic fetuses in the mail; the packages of fake anthrax; the glue in their locks; the Operation Rescue era, when sixty or seventy protesters would block their doors; the clinic bombing in Birmingham that killed a policeman and severely injured a nurse; the murder of Dr. Gunn; and the former policeman, recently on *Nightline*, who once said he thought he should have the right to shoot abortion doctors in the head. The last doctor here quit when all the personal information she gave to state officials suddenly appeared on abortiondocs.org, Ayres says. "It terrified her. She felt she had a target on her back and she just quit."

In this clinic, Parker's office is a storeroom filled with old chairs and traffic cones. He puts down his bag, abandons a plate of half-eaten eggs, and launches into a series of ultrasounds he feels are unnecessary—another mandate from the state. Each time, he begins with the same line: "The state requires me to repeat your ultrasound, so I'm going to do that."

In Mississippi, he says, they don't make you redo the ultrasound. In other states, they make you point out the fetal parts to the patient. It's pure harassment. The purpose is to "heighten the dilemma."

And so it does. The very first patient wants to know how far along she is.

"It is very small. Less than six weeks."

"Is there a fetal pole?" the patient asks.

"Are you a health-care professional?"

She's a nurse on a surgical-trauma team. She's here for officer's school.

"So you are air force?"

"Yes, sir."

When he tells her about the medication options, she shakes her head. "I am choosing to do it without the sedative," she says.

"That's fine. I'll be your sedative."

Patient after patient follows, thirty-four in all because the clinic hasn't had a doctor present for two weeks. Most of them have the same questions—how old the fetus is and whether they can have children in the future.

A woman named Monique asks if she gets a wish. Sure, Parker says.

"Please tell me that you can't find it."

"If only we could wish it away," he says.

Another woman tries to explain—she just got a promotion; she can't have a baby now.

"I hear ya. Life is full of those kinds of decisions."

One scan causes him to pause. "Do you want to know if there is more than one?" he asks.

The woman starts to cry. "No." She wipes away tears with both hands.

When she leaves, he points to the screen. Triplets. He's seen lots of twins but never triplets. Some women think multiples are more special, so they get more upset.

After another scan, he points at the tiny blob on the screen. Eighty-nine percent of pregnancies are that small or smaller at termination. "That's what we're fighting about. To people against abortion, that's a person. And that's more important than the woman."

When it's all over, he goes back to his storage closet and scoops down his cold eggs, then proceeds to a surgery room. The woman puts her feet in the stirrups and says, "I'm ready," and the door closes.

Right across is the recovery room, empty now. An elderly Black woman named Callie Chatman sits waiting for the women to emerge from surgery. She's a youth minister at a local Baptist church, where her husband is the pastor. She serves here as an exit counselor. "You know, preacher been teaching that the wages of sin is death," she says. "Not many of them know that God is a forgiving God. So if they ask me if I think they'll go to hell, I tell them what Jesus say: 'I do not condemn thee. Go and sin no more.' I tell them not to make the same mistake—and how not to make the same mistake."

Not one woman has told her that she thought abortion was okay, she adds. "What they have told me is it's the last resort. And I am here to let them know that God will meet you right where you are. And then I ask them to accept Christ as their lord and savior."

A couple women have accepted, she says, right here in the recovery room.

Now we arrive at the heart of the process, the focus of so much controversy and rage. In the surgical room, Dr. Parker softens each woman's cervix and uses a vacuum extractor to remove her pregnancy. The entire process takes five minutes. After each procedure, he carries the large glass vacuum bottle into an adjoining room. There he pours the fetal tissue from the bottle into an ordinary kitchen strainer and runs tap water over it, then empties the strainer into a clear Pyrex dish and examines the tissue on a light table.

Bending over the glass dish, he stares with the blank expression of a scientist at work. Come closer, he says. Have a look. These are blood clots and this is the decidual tissue, the stuff that looks like feathery coral. That supports the embryo, sloughing off monthly if a pregnancy doesn't develop.

This one is six weeks. It's just lumps of red tissue floating in water.

When the triplets arrive, he points out one sac, two sacs, three sacs.

But then he brings in one that's nine weeks and there's a fetus. He points out the scattered parts. "There's the skull, what is going to be the fetal skull. And there are the eye sockets."

Floating near the top of the dish are two tiny arms with two tiny hands.

Parker continues to examine the tissue. He points to a black spot the size of a pencil tip. "That's an eye."

"That black spot?"

"That black spot is an eye. And here's the umbilical cord."

The fetal pole has just begun to differentiate into a spine, but it still has a fishy tail of some kind of feathery material.

Very few outsiders are invited into this room, and rare is the doctor who would show this to a reporter. But today he made a conscious decision not to hide the truth. "At some point, we have to trust that people can deal with the reality of what this is," he says. "And keeping it hidden only enhances the stigma."

Growing reflective, he continues to study the parts. "The reality is we've disrupted a life process. There are recognizable fetal parts, right? The capacity for this development is always there. After five weeks, you just have the sac. At six weeks, you have a fetal pole with cardiac activity. At seven to eight weeks, it's just a larger fetal pole. By nine, it's differentiated."

But here's the vital question: Is it a person? Not by the standards of the law, he says. Is it viable outside the womb? It is not. So this piece of life—and remember, sperm is alive, eggs are alive, it's all life—is still totally dependent on a woman. And that dependence puts it in the domain of her choice. "That's what I embrace," he says.

But it's hard not to look at those tiny fingers, no bigger than the tip of a toothpick.

Does that ever disturb him?

"When I recognize whole fetal parts? No. Because I'm not deluded about what this whole process is."

And what does examining this tissue tell him? Does this satisfy another state regulation?

"It tells me her uterus is empty and she is no longer pregnant."

With that, Dr. Parker goes back into the operating room to give the woman who can now become an Air Force officer the sad good news.

When you look at the grim facts of climate change day after day for a living, immersing yourself in emission rates, melting ice, rising water, drought, and famine, a good night's sleep can be hard to come by.

T he incident was small, but Jason Box doesn't want to talk about it. He's been skittish about the media since it happened. This was last summer, as he was reading the cheery blog posts transmitted by the chief scientist on the Swedish icebreaker *Oden*, which was exploring the Arctic for an international expedition led by Stockholm University. "Our first observations of elevated methane levels, about ten times higher than in background seawater, were documented . . . we discovered over one hundred new methane seep sites . . . The weather Gods are still on our side as we steam through a now ice-free Laptev Sea . . . "

As a leading climatologist who spent many years studying the Arctic at the Byrd Polar and Climate Research Center at Ohio State, Box knew that this breezy scientific detachment described one of the nightmare long-shot climate scenarios: a feedback loop where warming seas release methane that causes warming that releases more methane that causes more warming, on and on until the planet is incompatible with human life. And he knew there were similar methane releases occurring in the area. On impulse, he sent out a tweet.

"If even a small fraction of Arctic sea floor carbon is released to the atmosphere, we're f'd."

The tweet immediately went viral, inspiring a series of headlines:

CLIMATOLOGIST SAYS ARCTIC CARBON RELEASE COULD MEAN "WE'RE FUCKED."

CLIMATE SCIENTIST DROPS THE F-BOMB AFTER STARTLING ARCTIC DISCOVERY.

CLIMATOLOGIST: METHANE PLUMES FROM THE ARCTIC MEAN WE'RE SCREWED.

Box has been outspoken for years. He's done science projects with Greenpeace, and he participated in the 2011 mass protest at the White House organized by 350.org. In 2013, he made headlines when a magazine reported his conclusion that a seventy-foot rise in sea levels over the next few centuries was probably already "baked into the system." Now, with one word, Box had ventured into two particularly dangerous areas. First, the dirty secret of climate science and government climate policies is that they're all based on probabilities, which means that the effects of standard CO_2 targets like an 80 percent reduction by 2050, are based on the middle of the probability curve. Box had ventured to the darker possibilities on the curve's tail, where few scientists and zero politicians are willing to go.

Worse, he showed emotion, a subject ringed with taboos in all science but especially in climate science. As a recent study from the University of Bristol documented, climate scientists have been so distracted and intimidated by the relentless campaign against them that they tend to avoid any statements that might get them labeled "alarmists," retreating into a world of charts and data. But Box had been able to resist all that. He even chased the media splash in interviews with the Danish press, where they translated "we're fucked" into its more decorous Danish equivalent, "on our ass," plastering those dispiriting words in large-type headlines all across the country.

The problem was that Box was now working for the Danish government, and even though Denmark may be the most progressive nation in the world on climate issues, its leaders still did not take kindly to one of its scientists distressing the populace with visions of global destruction. Convinced his job was in jeopardy only a year after he uprooted his young family and moved to a distant country, Box was summoned before the entire board of directors at his research institute. So now, when he gets an email asking for a phone call to discuss his "recent gloomy statements," he doesn't answer it.

Five days later: "Dr. Box—trying you again in case the message below went into your junk file. Please get in touch."

This time he responds briefly. "I think most scientists must be burying overt recognition of the awful truths of climate change in a protective layer of denial (not the same kind of denial coming from conservatives, of course). I'm still amazed how few climatologists have taken an advocacy message to the streets, demonstrating for some policy action." But he ignores the request for a phone call.

A week later, another try: "Dr. Box—I watched your speech at *The Economist*'s Arctic Summit. Wow. I would like to come see you."

But gloom is the one subject he doesn't want to discuss. "Crawling under a rock isn't an option," he responds, "so becoming overcome with PTSD-like symptoms is useless." He quotes a Norse proverb:

"The unwise man is awake all night, worries over and again. When morning rises he is restless still."

Most people don't have a proverb like that readily at hand. So, a final try: "I do think I should come to see you, meet your family, and make this story personal and vivid."

I wanted to meet Box to find out how this outspoken American is holding up. He has left his country and moved his family to witness and study the melting of Greenland up close. How does being the one to look at the grim facts of climate change most intimately, day in and day out, affect a person? Is Box representative of all of the scientists most directly involved in this defining issue of the new century? How are they being affected by the burden of their chosen work in the face of changes to the earth that could render it a different planet?

Finally, Box gives in. Come to Copenhagen, he says. And he even promises a family dinner.

For more than thirty years, climate scientists have been living a surreal existence. A vast and ever-growing body of research shows that warming is tracking the rise of greenhouse gases exactly as their models predicted. The physical evidence becomes more dramatic every year: forests retreating, animals moving north, glaciers melting, wildfire seasons getting longer, higher rates of droughts, floods, and storms—five times as many in the 2000s as in the 1970s. In the blunt words of the 2014 National Climate Assessment, conducted by three hundred of America's most distinguished experts at the request of the US government, human-induced climate change is real—US temperatures have gone up between 1.3 and 1.9 degrees, mostly since 1970—and the change is already affecting "agriculture, water, human health, energy, transportation, forests, and ecosystems." But that's not the worst of it. Arctic air temperatures are increasing at twice the rate of the rest of the world—a study by the US Navy says that the Arctic could lose its summer sea ice by next year, eighty-four years ahead of the models—and evidence little more than a year old suggests the West Antarctic Ice Sheet is doomed, which will add between twenty and twenty-five feet to ocean levels. The one hundred million people in Bangladesh will need another place to live and coastal cities globally will be forced to relocate, a task complicated by economic crisis and famine—with continental interiors drying out, the chief scientist at the US State Department in 2009 predicted a billion people will suffer famine within twenty or thirty years. And yet, despite some encouraging developments in renewable energy and some breakthroughs in international leadership, carbon emissions continue to rise at a steady rate, and for their pains the scientists themselves—the cruelest blow of all— have been the targets of an unrelenting and well-organized attack that includes death threats, summonses from a hostile Congress, attempts to get them fired, legal harassment, and intrusive discovery demands so severe they had to start their own legal-defense fund, all amplified by a relentless propaganda campaign nakedly financed by the fossil-fuel companies. Shortly before a pivotal climate summit in Copenhagen in 2009, thousands of their email streams were hacked in a sophisticated espionage operation that has never been solved—although the official police investigation revealed nothing, an analysis by forensics experts traced its path through servers in Turkey and two of the world's largest oil producers, Saudi Arabia and Russia.

Among climate activists, gloom is building. Jim Driscoll of the National Institute for Peer Support just finished a study of a group of longtime activists whose most frequently reported feeling was sadness, followed by fear and anger. Dr. Lise Van Susteren, a practicing psychiatrist and graduate of Al Gore's Inconvenient Truth slide-show training, calls this "pretraumatic" stress. "So many of us are exhibiting all the signs and symptoms of posttraumatic disorder—the anger, the panic, the obsessive intrusive thoughts." Leading activist Gillian Caldwell went public with her "climate trauma," as she called it, quitting the group she helped build and posting an article called "16 Tips for Avoiding Climate Burnout," in which she suggests compartmentalization: "Reinforce boundaries between professional work and personal life. It is very hard to switch from the riveting force of apocalyptic predictions at work to home, where the problems are petty by comparison."

Most of the dozens of scientists and activists I spoke to date the rise of the melancholy mood to the failure of the 2009 climate conference and the gradual shift from hope of prevention to plans for adaptation: Bill McKibben's book *Eaarth* is a manual for survival on an earth so different he doesn't think we should even spell it the same, and James Lovelock delivers the same message in *A Rough Ride to the Future*. In Australia, Clive Hamilton writes articles and books with titles like *Requiem for a Species*. In a recent issue of the *New Yorker*, the melancholy Jonathan Franzen argued that, since earth now "resembles a patient whose terminal cancer we can choose to treat either with disfiguring aggression or with palliation and sympathy," we should stop trying to avoid the inevitable and spend our money on new nature preserves, where birds can go extinct a little more slowly.

At the darkest end of the spectrum are groups like Deep Green Resistance, which openly advocates sabotage to "industrial infrastructure," and the thousands who visit the website and attend the speeches of Guy McPherson, a biology professor at the University of Arizona who concluded that renewables would do no good, left his job, and moved to an off-grid homestead to prepare for abrupt climate change. "Civilization is a heat engine," he says. "There's no escaping the trap we've landed ourselves into."

The most influential is Paul Kingsnorth, a longtime climate activist and novelist who abandoned hope for political change in 2009. Retreating to the woods of western Ireland, he helped launch a group called Dark Mountain with a stirring, gloomy manifesto calling for "a network of writers, artists, and thinkers who have stopped believing the stories our civilization tells itself." Among those stories: progress, growth, and the superiority of man. The idea quickly spread, and there are now fifty Dark Mountain chapters around the world. Fans have written plays and songs and a PhD thesis about them. On the phone from Ireland, he explains the appeal.

"You have to be careful about hope. If that hope is based on an unrealistic foundation, it just crumbles and then you end up with people who are despairing. I saw that in Copenhagen—there was a lot of despair and giving up after that."

Personally, though he considers them feeble gestures, he's planting a lot of trees, growing his own vegetables, avoiding plastic. He stopped flying. "It seems like an ethical obligation. All you can do is what you think is right." The odd thing is that he's much more forgiving than activists still in the struggle, even with oil-purchased politicians. "We all love the fruits of what we're given—the cars and computers and iPhones. What politician is going to try to sell people a future where they can't update their iPhones *ever*?"

He laughs.

Does he think it would be wrong to take a transatlantic airplane trip to interview a climate scientist?

He laughs again. "You have to answer that yourself."

All this leaves climate scientists in an awkward position. At NASA's Goddard Institute for Space Studies, which early in the year was threatened with 30 percent budget cuts by Republicans who resent its reports on climate change, Gavin Schmidt occupies the seventh-floor corner office once occupied by the legendary James Hansen, the scientist who first laid out the facts for Congress in 1988 and grew so impassioned he got himself arrested protesting coal mines. Although Schmidt was one of the victims of the 2009 computer hacks, which he admits tipped him into an episode of serious depression, he now focuses relentlessly on the bright side. "It's not that nothing has been done. There's a lot of things. In terms of per capita emissions, most of the developed world is stable. So we are doing *something*."

Box's tweet sets his teeth on edge. "I don't agree. I don't think we're fucked. There is time to build sustainable solutions to a lot of these things. You don't have to close down all the coal-powered stations tomorrow. You can transition. It sounds cute to say, 'Oh, we're fucked and there's nothing we can do,' but it's a bit of a nihilistic attitude. We always have the choice. We can continue to make worse decisions, or we can try to make ever better decisions. 'Oh, we're fucked! Just give up now, just kill me now,' that's just stupid."

Schmidt, who is expecting his first child and tries to live a low-carbon existence, insists that the hacks and investigations and budget threats have not intimidated him. He also shrugs off the abrupt-climate-change scenarios. "The methane thing is actually something I work on a lot, and most of the headlines are crap. There's no actual evidence that anything dramatically different is going on in the Arctic, other than the fact that it's melting pretty much everywhere."

But climate change happens gradually and we've already gone up almost one degree centigrade and seen eight inches of ocean rise. Barring unthinkably radical change, we'll hit two degrees in thirty or forty years and that's been described as a catastrophe—melting ice, rising waters, drought, famine, and massive economic turmoil. And many scientists now think we're on track to four or five degrees— even Shell oil said that it anticipates a world four degrees hotter because it doesn't see "governments taking the steps now that are consistent with the two degrees C scenario." That would mean a world racked by economic and social and environmental collapse.

"Oh yeah," Schmidt says, almost casually. "The business-as-usual world that we project is really a totally different planet. There's going to be huge dislocations if that comes about."

But things can change much quicker than people think, he says. Look at attitudes on gay marriage.

And the glaciers?

"The glaciers are going to melt, they're all going to melt," he says. "But my reaction to Jason Box's comments is—what is the point of saying that? It doesn't help anybody."

As it happens, Schmidt was the first winner of the Climate Communication Prize from the American Geophysical Union, and various recent studies in the growing field of climate communications find that frank talk about the grim realities turns people off—it's simply too much to take in. But strategy is one thing and truth is another. Aren't those glaciers water sources for hundreds of millions of people?

"Particularly in the Indian subcontinent, that's a real issue," he says. "There's going to be dislocation there, no question."

And the rising oceans? Bangladesh is almost underwater now. Do a hundred million people have to move?

"Well, yeah. Under business as usual. But I don't think we're fucked."

Resource wars, starvation, mass migrations . . .

"Bad things are going to happen. What can you do as a person? You write stories. I do science. You don't run around saying, 'We're fucked! We're fucked! We're fucked!' It doesn't—it doesn't incentivize anybody to *do* anything."

Scientists are problem solvers by nature, trained to cherish detachment as a moral ideal. Jeffrey Kiehl was a senior scientist with the National Center for Atmospheric Research when he became so concerned about the way the brain resists climate science, he took a break and got a psychology degree. Ten years of research later, he's concluded that consumption and growth have become so central to our sense of personal identity and the fear of economic loss creates such numbing anxiety, we literally cannot imagine making the necessary changes. Worse, accepting the facts threatens us with a loss of faith in the fundamental order of the universe. Climate scientists are different only because they have a professional excuse for detachment, and usually it's not until they get older that they admit how much it's affecting them—which is also when they tend to get more outspoken, Kiehl says. "You reach a point where you feel—and that's the word, not *think*, *feel*—'I have to do something.'"

This accounts for the startled reaction when Camille Parmesan of the University of Texas—who was a member of the group that shared a Nobel prize with Al Gore for their climate work—announced that she'd become "professionally depressed" and was leaving the United States for England. A plainspoken Texan who grew up in Houston as the daughter of an oil geologist, Parmesan now says it was more about the politics than the science. "To be honest, I panicked fifteen years ago—that was when the first studies came out showing that Arctic tundras were shifting from being a net sink to being a net source of CO_2. That along with the fact this butterfly I was studying shifted its entire range across half a continent—I said this is big, this is big. Everything since then has just confirmed it."

But she's not optimistic. "Do I think it likely that the nations of the world will take sufficient action to stabilize climate in the next fifty years? No, I don't think it likely."

She was living in Texas after the climate summit failed in 2009, when media coverage of climate issues plunged by two thirds—the subject wasn't mentioned once in the 2012 presidential debates—and Governor Rick Perry cut the sections relating to sea-level rise in a report on Galveston Bay, kicking off a trend of state officials who ban all use of the term "climate change." "There are excellent climate scientists in Texas," Parmesan says firmly. "Every university in the state has people working on impacts. To have the governor's office ignore it is just very upsetting."

The politics took its toll. Her butterfly study got her a spot on the UN climate panel, where she got "a quick and hard lesson on the politics" when policymakers killed the words "high confidence" in the crucial passage that said scientists had high confidence species were responding to climate change. Then the personal attacks started on right-wing websites and blogs. "They just flat-out lie. It's one reason I live in the UK now. It's not just been climate change, there's a growing, ever-stronger antiscience sentiment in the USA. People get really angry and really nasty. It was a huge relief simply not to have to deal with it." She now advises her graduate students to look for jobs outside the US.

No one has experienced that hostility more vividly than Michael Mann, who was a young PhD researcher when he helped come up with the historical data that came to be known as the hockey stick—the most incendiary display graph in human history, with its temperature and emissions lines going straight up at the end like the blade of a hockey stick. He was investigated, was denounced in Congress, got death threats, was accused of fraud, received white powder in the mail, and got thousands of emails with suggestions like, You should be "shot, quartered, and fed to the pigs along with your whole damn families." Conservative legal foundations pressured his university, a British journalist suggested the electric chair. In 2003, Senator James Inhofe's committee called him to testify, flanking him with two professional climate-change deniers, and in 2011 the committee threatened him with federal prosecution, along with sixteen other scientists.

Now, sitting behind his desk in his office at Penn State, he goes back to his swirl of emotions. "You find yourself in the center of this political theater, in this chess match that's being played out by very powerful figures—you feel anger, befuddlement, disillusionment, disgust."

The intimidating effect is undeniable, he says. Some of his colleagues were so demoralized by the accusations and investigations that they withdrew from public life. One came close to suicide. Mann decided to fight back, devoting more of his time to press interviews and public speaking, and discovered that contact with other concerned people always cheered him up. But the sense of potential danger never leaves. "You're careful with what you say and do because you know that there's the equivalent of somebody with a movie camera following you around," he says.

Meanwhile, his sense of personal alarm has only grown. "I know you've spoken with Jason Box—a number of us have had these experiences where it's become clear to us that in many respects, climate change is unfolding faster than we expected it to. Maybe it is true what the ice-sheet modelers have been telling us, that it will take a thousand years or more to melt the Greenland Ice Sheet. But maybe they're wrong; maybe it could play out in a century or two. And then it's a whole different ballgame—it's the difference between human civilization and living things being able to adapt and not being able to adapt."

As Mann sees it, scientists like Schmidt who choose to focus on the middle of the curve aren't really being scientific. Worse are pseudo-sympathizers like Bjorn Lomborg who always focus on the gentlest possibilities. Because we're supposed to hope for the best and prepare for the worst, and a real scientific response would also give serious weight to the dark side of the curve.

And yet, like Schmidt, Mann tries very hard to look on the bright side. We can solve this problem in a way that doesn't disrupt our lifestyle, he says. Public awareness seems to be increasing, and there are a lot of good things happening at the executive level: tighter fuel-efficiency standards, the carbon-pricing initiatives by the New England and West Coast states, the recent agreement between the US and China on emissions. Last year we saw global economic growth without an increase in carbon emissions, which suggests it's possible to "decouple" oil and economic growth. And social change can happen very fast—look at gay marriage.

But he knows that gay marriage had no huge economic downside, and the most powerful companies in the world are fighting to stop any change in the fossil-fuel economy. So yes, he struggles with doubt. And he admits that some of his colleagues are very depressed, convinced there's no way the international community will rise to the challenge. He gets into that conversation in bars after climate conferences, always pushing the side of hope.

Dealing with all of this has been along emotional journey. As a young scientist, Mann was very traditional: "I felt that scientists should take an entirely dispassionate view when discussing matters of science," he wrote in a book called *The Hockey Stick and the Climate Wars*. "We should do our best to divorce ourselves from all of our typically human inclinations—emotion, empathy, concern." But even when he decided that detachment was a mistake in this case and began becoming publicly active, he was usually able to put the implication of all the hockey-stick trend lines out of his mind. "Part of being a scientist is you don't want to believe there is a problem you can't solve."

Might that be just another form of denial?

The question seems to affect him. He takes a deep breath and answers in the carefully measured words of a scientist. "It's hard to say," he says. "It's a denial of futility if there is futility. But I don't know that there is futility, so it would only be denial per se if there were unassailable evidence."

There are moments, he admits, flashes that come and go as fast as a blinking light, when he sees news reports about some new development in the field and it hits him—Wait a second, they're saying that we've melted a *lot*. Then he does a peculiar thing: He disassociates a little bit and asks himself, How would I feel about that headline if I were a member of the public? I'd be scared *out of my mind*.

Right after Hurricane Sandy, he was in the classroom showing *The Day After Tomorrow* with the plan of critiquing its ridiculous story about the Atlantic conveyor belt slowing down so fast that it freezes England—except a recent study he worked on shows that the Atlantic conveyor belt actually is slowing down, another thing that's happening decades ahead of schedule. "And some of the scenes in the wake of Hurricane Sandy—the flooding of the New York City subway system, cars submerged—they really didn't look that different. The cartoon suddenly looked less like a cartoon. And it's like, Now why is it that we can completely dismiss this movie?"

He was talking to students, so it got to him. They're young, it's their future more than his. He choked up and had to struggle to get ahold of himself. "You don't want to choke up in front of your class," he says.

About once a year, he says, he has nightmares of earth becoming a very alien planet.

The worst time was when he was reading his daughter Dr. Seuss's *The Lorax*, the story of a society destroyed by greed. He saw it as an optimistic story because it ends with the challenge of building a new society, but she burst into tears and refused to read the book again. "It was almost traumatic for her."

"I don't want her to have to be sad," he says. "And I almost *have* to believe we're not yet there, where we are resigned to this future."

The spring day is glorious, sunny and cool, and the avenues of Copenhagen are alive with tourists. Trying to make the best of things, Jason Box says we should blow off the getting-to-know-you lunch and go for a bike ride. Thirty minutes later he locks up the bikes at the entrance to Freetown, a local anarchist community that has improbably become one of Copenhagen's most popular tourist destinations. Grabbing a couple beers at a restaurant, he leads the way to a winding lake and a small dock. The wind is blowing, swans flap their wings just off the beach, and Box sits with the sun on his face and his feet dangling over the sand.

"There's a lot that's scary," he says, running down the list—the melting sea ice, the slowing of the conveyor belt. Only in the last few years were they able to conclude that Greenland is warmer than it was in the twenties, and the unpublished data looks very hockey-stick-ish. He figures there's a 50 percent chance we're already committed to going beyond two degrees centigrade and agrees with the growing consensus that the business-as-usual trajectory is four or five degrees. "It's, um . . . bad. Really nasty."

The big question is, What amount of warming puts Greenland into irreversible loss? That's what will destroy all the coastal cities on earth. The answer is between two and three degrees. "Then it just thins and thins enough and you can't regrow it without an ice age. And a small fraction of that is already a huge problem—Florida's already installing all these expensive pumps." (According to a recent report by a group spearheaded by Hank Paulson and Robert Rubin, secretaries of the Treasury under Bush Jr. and Bill Clinton, respectively, $23 billion worth of property in Florida may be destroyed by flooding within thirty-five years.)

Box is only forty-two, but his pointed Danish beard makes him look like a count in an old novel, someone who'd wear a frock coat and say something droll about the woman question. He seems detached from the sunny day, like a tourist trying to relax in a strange city. He also seems oddly detached from the things he's saying, laying out one horrible prediction after another without emotion, as if he were an anthropologist regarding the life cycle of a distant civilization. But he can't keep his anger in check for long and keeps obsessively returning to two topics:

"We need the deniers to get out of the way. They are risking everyone's future. . . . The Koch Brothers are criminals. . . . They should be charged with criminal activity because they're putting the profits of their business ahead of the livelihoods of millions of people, and even life on earth."

Like Parmesan, Box was hugely relieved to be out of the toxic atmosphere of the US. "I remember thinking, What a relief, I don't have to bother with this bullshit anymore." In Denmark, his research is supported through the efforts of conservative politicians. "But Danish conservatives are not climate-change deniers," he says.

The other topic he is obsessed with is the human suffering to come. Long before the rising waters from Greenland's glaciers displace the desperate millions, he says more than once, we will face drought-triggered agricultural failures and water-security issues—in fact, it's already happening. Think back to the 2010 Russian heat wave. Moscow halted grain exports. At the peak of the Australian drought, food prices spiked. The Arab Spring started with food protests, the self-immolation of the vegetable vendor in Tunisia. The Syrian conflict was preceded by four years of drought. Same with Darfur. The migrants are already starting to stream north across the sea—just yesterday, eight hundred of them died when their boat capsized—and the Europeans are arguing about what to do with them. "As the Pentagon says, climate change is a conflict multiplier."

His home state of Colorado isn't doing so great, either. "The forests are dying, and they will not return. The trees won't return to a warming climate. We're going to see megafires even more, that'll be the new one—megafires until those forests are cleared."

However dispassionately delivered, all of this amounts to a lament, the scientist's version of the mothers who stand on hillsides and keen over the death of their sons. In fact, Box adds, he too is a climate refugee. His daughter is three and a half, and Denmark is a great place to be in an uncertain world—there's plenty of water, a high-tech agriculture system, increasing adoption of wind power, and plenty of geographic distance from the coming upheavals. "Especially when you consider the beginning of the flood of desperate people from conflict and drought," he says, returning to his obsession with how profoundly changed our civilization will be.

Despite all this, he insists that he approaches climate mostly as an intellectual problem. For the first decade of his career, even though he's part of the generation of climate scientists who went to college after Al Gore's *Earth in the Balance*, he stuck to teaching and research. He only began taking professional risks by working with Greenpeace and by joining the protest against Keystone when he came to the intellectual conclusion that climate change is a moral issue. "It's unethical to bankrupt the environment of this planet," he says. "That's a tragedy, right?" Even now, he insists, the horror of what is happening rarely touches him on an emotional level . . . although it has been hitting him more often recently. "But I—I—I'm not letting it get to me. If I spend my energy on despair, I won't be thinking about opportunities to minimize the problem."

His insistence on this point is very unconvincing, especially given the solemnity that shrouds him like a dark coat. But the most interesting part is the insistence itself—the desperate need not to be disturbed by something so disturbing. Suddenly, a welcome distraction. A man appears on the beach in nothing but jockey shorts, his skin bluish. He says he's Greek and he's been sleeping on this beach for seven months and will swim across the lake for a small tip. A passing tourist asks if he can swim all the way.

"Of course."

"Let me see."

"How much money?"

"I give you when you get back."

"Give me one hundred."

"Yeah, yeah. When you get back."

The Greek man splashes into the water and Box seems amused, laughing for the first time. It's the relief of normal goofy human life, so distant from the dark themes that make up his life's work.

Usually it's a scientific development that smacks him, he says. The first was in 2002, when they discovered that meltwater was getting into the bed of the Greenland Ice Sheet and lubricating its flow. Oh, you say, it can be a wet bed, and then the implications sunk in: *The whole damn thing is destabilizing.* Then in 2006, all of the glaciers in the southern half of Greenland began to retreat at two and three times their previous speed. *Good Lord, it's happening so fast.* Two years later, they realized the retreat was fueled by warm water eroding the marine base ice—which is also what's happening to the West Antarctic Ice Sheet. Just thinking about it makes him gloomy. "That's unstoppable," he says. "Abrupt sea-level rise is upon us."

The Greek man returns with surprising speed, emerging from the sea like a god in a myth, laughing and boasting. The Greeks are masters of the waters! Pay me!

"I'm gonna give this guy a hundred kroner," Box says.

He makes sure the tourists pay, too, and comes back smiling. He knows a Greek guy who's just like that, he says, very proud and jolly. He envies him sometimes.

He leads the way to a quieter spot on the lakeside, passing through little hippie villages woven together by narrow dirt lanes— by consensus vote, there are no cars in Freetown, which makes it feel pleasantly medieval, intimate, and human-scaled. He lifts a beer to his lips and gazes over the lake and the happy people lazing in the afternoon sun. "The question of despair is not very nice to think about," he says. "I've just disengaged that to a large degree. It's kind of like a half-denial."

He mentions the Norse proverb again, but a bulwark against despair so often cited becomes its own form of despair. You don't dredge up proverbs like that unless you're staying awake at night.

He nods, sighing. This work often disturbs his sleep, driving him from his bed to do something, anything. "Yeah, the shit that's going down has been testing my ability to block it."

He goes quiet for a moment. "It certainly does creep in, as a parent," he says quietly, his eyes to the ground.

But let's get real, he says, fossil fuels are the dominant industry on earth, and you can't expect meaningful political change with them in control. "There's a growing consensus that there must be a shock to the system."

So the darker hopes arise—maybe a particularly furious EL Nino or a "carbon bubble" where the financial markets realize that renewables have become more scalable and economical, leading to a run on fossil-fuel assets and a "generational crash" of the global economy that, through great suffering, buys us more time and forces change.

The Box family dinner isn't going to happen after all, he says. When it comes to climate change at the very late date of 2015, there are just too many uncomfortable things to say, and his wife, Klara, resents any notion that she is a "climate migrant."

This is the first hint that his brashness has caused tension at home.

"Well, she . . . " He takes a moment, considering. "I'll say something like, 'Man, the next twenty years are going to be a hell of a ride,' or 'These poor North African refugees flooding to Europe,' and how I anticipate that flux of people to double and triple, and will the open borders of Europe change? And she'll acknowledge it . . . but she's not bringing it up like I am."

Later, she sends a note responding to a few questions. She didn't want to compare herself to the truly desperate refugees who are drowning, she says, and the move to Denmark really was for the quality of life. "Lastly, the most difficult question to answer is about Jason's mental health. I'd say climate change, and more broadly the whole host of environmental and social problems the world faces, does affect his psyche. He feels deeply about these issues, but he is a scientist and a very pragmatic, goal-oriented person. His style is not to lie awake at night worrying about them but to get up in the morning (or the middle of the night) and do something about it. I love the guy for it :) "

So even when you are driven to your desk in the middle of the night, quoting Norse proverbs, when you are among the most informed and most concerned, the ordinary tender mercies of the home conspire in our denial. We pour our energy into doing our jobs the best we can, avoid unpleasant topics, keep up a brave face, make compromises with even the best societies, and little by little the compartmentalization we need to survive the day adds one more bit of distance between the comfortable now and the horrors ahead. So Box turns out to be a representative figure after all. It's not enough to understand the changes that are coming. We have to find a way to live with them.

"In Denmark," Box says, "we have the resilience, so I'm not that worried about my daughter's livelihood going forward. But that doesn't stop me from strategizing about how to safeguard her future—I've been looking at property in Greenland. As a possible bug-out scenario."

Turns out a person can't own land in Greenland, just a house on top of land. It's a nice thought, a comforting thought—no matter what happens, the house will be there, safely hidden at the top of the world.

CHILDREN
OF TED

In the decades since his last deadly act of ecoterrorism, the Unabomber has become an unlikely prophet to a whole new generation of young acolytes. And what does Ted Kaczynski say? "The political situation is complex and could be discussed endlessly," he tells me, "but for now I will only say this — the current political turmoil provides an environment in which a revolutionary movement should be able to gain a foothold."

When John Jacobi stepped to the altar of his Pentecostal church and the gift of tongues seized him, his mother heard prophecies—just a child and already blessed, she said. Someday, surely, her angelic blond boy would bring a light to the world, and maybe she wasn't wrong. His quest began early. When he was five, the Alabama child-welfare workers decided that his mother's boyfriend—a drug dealer named Rock who had a red carpet leading to his trailer and plaster lions standing guard at the door—wasn't providing a suitable environment for John and his sisters and little brother. Before they knew it, they were living with their father, an army officer stationed in Fayetteville, North Carolina. But two years later, when he was posted to Iraq, the social workers shipped the kids back to Alabama, where they stayed until their mother hanged herself from a tree in the yard. John was fourteen. In the tumultuous years that followed, he lost his faith, wrote mournful poems, took an interest in news reports about a lively new protest movement called Occupy Wall Street, and ran away from the home of the latest relative who'd taken him in—just for a night, but that was enough. As soon as he graduated from high school, he quit his job at McDonald's, bought some camping gear, and set out in search of a better world.

When a young American lights out for the territories in the second decade of the twenty-first century, where does he go? For John Jacobi, the answer was Chapel Hill, North Carolina—Occupy had gotten him interested in anarchists, and he'd heard they were active there. He was camping out with the chickens in the backyard of their communal headquarters a few months later when a crusty old anarchist with dreadlocks and a piercing gaze handed him a dog-eared book called *Industrial Society and Its Future*. The author was FC, whoever that was. Jacobi glanced at the first line: "The Industrial Revolution and its consequences have been a disaster for the human race."

This guy sure gets to the point, he thought. He skimmed down the paragraph. Industrial society has caused "widespread psychological suffering" and "severe damage to the natural world"? Made life more comfortable in rich countries but miserable in the Third World? That sounded right to him. He found a quiet nook and read on.

The book was written in 232 numbered sections, like an instruction manual for some immense tool. There were two main themes. First, we've become so dependent on technology that the real decisions about our lives are made by unseen forces like corporations and market flows. Our lives are "modified to fit the needs of this system," and the diseases of modern life are the result: "Boredom, demoralization, low self-esteem, inferiority feelings, defeatism, depression, anxiety, guilt, frustration, hostility, spouse or child abuse, insatiable hedonism, abnormal sexual behavior, sleep disorders, eating disorders, etc." Jacobi had experienced most of those himself.

The second point was that technology's dark momentum can't be stopped. With each improvement, the graceful schooner that sails our shorelines becomes the hulking megatanker that takes our jobs. The car's a blast bouncing along at the reckless speed of 20 mph, but pretty soon we're buying insurance, producing our license and registration if we fail to obey posted signs, and cursing when one of those charming behavior-modification devices in orange envelopes shows up on our windshields. We doze off while exploring a fun new thing called social media and wake up to big data, fake news, and Total Information Awareness.

All true, Jacobi thought. *Who the hell wrote this thing?*

The clue arrived in section No. 96: "In order to get our message before the public with some chance of making a lasting impression, we've had to kill people," the mystery author wrote.

"Kill people"—Jacobi realized that he was reading the words of the Unabomber, Ted Kaczynski, the hermit who sent mail bombs to scientists, executives, and computer experts beginning in 1978. FC stood for Freedom Club, the pseudonym Kaczynski used to take credit for his attacks. He said he'd stop if the newspapers published his manifesto, and they did, which is how he got caught, in 1995—his brother recognized his prose style and reported him to the FBI. Jacobi flipped back to the first page, section No. 4: "We therefore advocate a revolution against the industrial system."

The first time he read that passage, Jacobi had just nodded along. Talking about revolution was the anarchist version of praising the baby Jesus, invoked so frequently it faded into background noise. But Kaczynski meant it. He was a genius who went to Harvard at sixteen and made breakthroughs in something called "boundary functions" in his twenties. He joined the mathematics department at UC Berkeley when he was twenty-five, the youngest hire in the university's then-ninety-nine-year history. And he did try to escape the world he could no longer bear by moving to Montana. He lived in peace without electricity or running water until the day when, maddened by the invasion of cars and chain saws and people, he hiked to his favorite wild place for some relief and found a road cut through it. "You just can't imagine how upset I was," he told an interviewer in 1999. "From that point on, I decided that, rather than trying to acquire further wilderness skills, I would work on getting back at the system. Revenge." In the next seventeen years, he killed three people and wounded twenty-three more.

Jacobi didn't know most of those details yet, but he couldn't find any holes in Kaczynski's logic. He said straight-out that ordinary human beings would never charge the barricades, shouting, "Destroy our way of life! Plunge us into a desperate struggle for survival!" They'd probably just stagger along, patching holes and destroying the planet, which meant "a small core of deeply committed people" would have to do the job themselves (section No. 189). Kaczynski even offered tactical advice in an essay titled "Hit Where It Hurts," published a few years after he began his life sentence in a federal "supermax" prison in Colorado: Forget the small targets and attack critical infrastructure like electric grids and communication networks. Take down a few of those at the right time and the ripples would spread rapidly, crashing the global economic system and giving the planet a breather: No more CO_2 pumped into the atmosphere, no more iPhones tracking our every move, no more robots taking our jobs.

Kaczynski was just as unsentimental about the downsides. Sure, decades or centuries after the collapse, we might crawl out of the rubble and get back to a simpler, freer way of life, without money or debt, in harmony with nature instead of trying to fight it. But before that happened, there was likely to be "great suffering"—violent clashes over resources, mass starvation, the rise of warlords. The way Kaczynski saw it, though, the longer we go like we're going, the worse things will get. At the time his manifesto was published, many people reading it probably hadn't heard of global warming and most certainly weren't worried about it. Reading it in 2014 was a very different experience.

The shock that went through Jacobi in that moment—you could call it his "Kaczynski Moment"—made the idea of destroying civilization real. And if Kaczynski was right, wouldn't he have some responsibility to do something, to sabotage one of those electric grids?

His answer was yes, which was almost as alarming as discovering an unexpected kinship with a serial killer—even when you're sure that morality is just a social construct that keeps us docile in our shearing pens, it turns out setting off a chain of events that could kill a lot of people can raise a few qualms.

"But by then," Jacobi says, "I was already hooked."

Quietly, often secretly, whether they gather it from the air of this anxious era or directly from the source like Jacobi did, more and more people have been having Kaczynski Moments. Books and webzines with names like *Against Civilization*, FeralCulture, Unsettling America, and the Ludd-Kaczynski Institute of Technology have been spreading versions of his message across social-media forums from Reddit to Facebook for at least a decade, some attracting more than one hundred thousand followers. They cluster around a youthful nickname, "anti-civ," some drawing their ideas directly from Kaczynski, others from movements like deep ecology, anarchy, primitivism, and nihilism, mixing them into new strains. Although they all believe industrial civilization is in a death spiral, most aren't trying to hurry it along. One exception is Deep Green Resistance, an activist network inspired by a 2011 book of the same name that includes contributions from one of Kaczynski's frequent correspondents, Derrick Jensen. The group's openly stated goal, like Kaczynski's, is the destruction of civilization and a return to preagricultural ways of life.

So far, most of the violence has happened outside of the United States. Although the FBI declined to comment on the topic, the 2017 report on domestic terrorism by the Congressional Research Service cited just a handful of minor attacks on "symbols of Western civilization" in the past ten years, a period of relative calm most credit to Operation Backfire, the FBI crackdown on radical environmental efforts in the mid-aughts. But in Latin America and Europe, terrorist groups with florid names like Conspiracy of Cells of Fire and Wild Indomitables have been bombing government buildings and assassinating technologists for almost a decade. The most ominous example is Individualidades Tendiendo a lo Salvaje, or ITS (usually translated as Individuals Tending Toward the Wild), a loose association of terrorist groups started by Mexican Kaczynski devotees who decided that his plan to take down the system was outdated because the environment was being decimated so fast and government surveillance technology had gotten so robust. Instead, ITS would return to its guru's old modus operandi: revenge. The group set off bombs at the National Ecology Institute in Mexico, a Federal Electricity Commission office, two banks, and a university. It now claims cells across Latin America, and in January 2017, the Chilean offshoot delivered a gift-wrapped bomb to Oscar Landerretche, the chairman of the world's largest copper mine, who suffered minor injuries. The group explained its motives in a defiant media release: "The pretentious Landerretche deserved to die for his offenses against Earth."

In the larger world, where no respectable person would praise Kaczynski without denouncing his crimes, little Kaczynski Moments have been popping up in the most unexpected places—the Fox News website, for example, which ran a piece by Keith Ablow called "Was the Unabomber Correct?" in 2013. After summarizing some of Kaczynski's dark predictions about the steady erosion of individual autonomy in a world where the tools and systems that create prosperity are too complex for any normal person to understand, Ablow—Fox's "expert on psychiatry"—came to the conclusion that Kaczynski was "precisely correct in many of his ideas" and even something of a prophet. "Watching the development of Facebook heighten the narcissism of tens of millions of people, turning them into mini reality-TV versions of themselves," he wrote. "I would bet he knows, with even more certainty, that he was onto something."

That same year, in the leading environmentalist journal *Orion*, a "recovering environmentalist" named Paul Kingsnorth—who'd stunned his fellow activists in 2008 by announcing that he'd lost hope—published an essay about the disturbing experience of reading Kaczynski's manifesto for the first time. If he ended up agreeing with Kaczynski, "I'm worried that it may change my life," he confessed. "Not just in the ways I've already changed it (getting rid of my telly, not owning a credit card, avoiding smartphones and e-readers and sat-navs, growing at least some of my own food, learning practical skills, fleeing the city, etc.) but properly, deeply."

By 2017, Kaczynski was making inroads with the conservative intelligentsia—in the journal *First Things*, home base for neocons like Midge Decter and theologians like Michael Novak, deputy editor Elliot Milco described his reaction to the manifesto in an article called "Searching for Ted Kaczynski": "What I found in the text, and in letters written by Kaczynski since his incarceration, was a man with a large number of astute (even prophetic) insights into American political life and culture. Much of his thinking would be at home in the pages of *First Things*." A year later, *Foreign Policy* published "The Next Wave of Extremism Will Be Green," an editorial written by Jamie Bartlett, a British journalist who tracks the anti-civ movement. He estimated that a "few thousand" Americans were already prepared to commit acts of destruction. Citing examples such as the Standing Rock pipeline protests in 2017, Bartlett wrote, "The necessary conditions for the radicalization of climate activism are all in place. Some groups are already showing signs of making the transition."

The fear of technology seems to grow every day. Tech tycoons build bug-out estates in New Zealand, smartphone executives refuse to let their kids use smartphones, data miners find ways to hide their own data. We entertain ourselves with *I Am Legend*, *The Road*, *V for Vendetta*, and *Avatar* while our kids watch *Wall-E* or *FernGully: The Last Rainforest*. An eight-part docudrama called *Manhunt: The Unabomber* was a hit when it premiered on the Discovery Channel in 2017 and a "super hit" when Netflix rereleased it last summer, says Elliott Halpern, the producer Netflix commissioned to make another film focusing on Kaczynski's "ideas and legacy." "Obviously," Halpern says, "he predicted a lot of stuff."

And wouldn't you know it, Kaczynski's papers have become one of the most popular attractions at the University of Michigan's Labadie Collection, an archive of original documents from movements of "social unrest." Kaczynski's archivist, Julie Herrada, couldn't say much about the people who visit—the archive has a policy against characterizing its clientele—but she did offer a word in their defense. "Nobody seems crazy."

Two years ago, I started trading letters with Kaczynski. His responses are relentlessly methodical and laced with footnotes, but he seems to have a droll side, too. "Thank you for your undated letter postmarked 6/11/18, but you wrote the address so sloppily that I'm surprised the letter reached me . . . " "Thank you for your letter of 8/6/18, which I received on 8/16/18. It looks like a more elaborate and better developed, but otherwise typical, example of the type of brown-nosing that journalists send to a 'mark' to get him to cooperate." Questions that revealed unfamiliarity with his work were poorly received. "It seems that most big-time journalists are incapable of understanding what they read and incapable of transmitting facts accurately. They are frustrated fiction-writers, not fact-oriented people." I tried to warm him up with samples of my brilliant prose. "Dear John, Johnny, Jack, Mr. Richardson, or whatever," he began, before informing me that my writing reminded him of something the editor of another magazine told the social critic Paul Goodman, as recounted in Goodman's book *Growing Up Absurd*: "'If you mean to tell me,' an editor said to me, 'that *Esquire* tries to have articles on serious issues and treats them in such a way that nothing can come of it, who can deny it?'" (Kaczynski's characteristically scrupulous footnote adds a caveat, "Quoted from memory.") His response to a question about his political preferences was extra dry: "It's certainly an oversimplification to say that the struggle between left & right in America today is a struggle between the neurotics and the sociopaths (left = neurotics, right = sociopaths = criminal types)," he said, "but there is nevertheless a good deal of truth in that statement."

But the jokes came to an abrupt stop when I asked for his take on America's descent into immobilizing partisan warfare. "The political situation is complex and could be discussed endlessly, but for now I will only say this," he answered. "The current political turmoil provides an environment in which a revolutionary movement should be able to gain a foothold." He returned to the point later with more enthusiasm: "Present situation looks a lot like situation (19th century) leading up to Russian Revolution, or (pre-1911) to Chinese Revolution. You have all these different factions, mostly goofy and unrealistic, and in disagreement if not in conflict with one another, but all agreeing that the situation is intolerable and that change of the most radical kind is necessary and inevitable. To this mix add one leader of genius."

Kaczynski was Karl Marx in modern flesh, yearning for his Lenin. In my next letter, I asked if any candidates had approached him. His answer was an impatient no—obviously any revolutionary stupid enough to write to him would be too stupid to lead a revolution. "Wait, I just thought of an exception: John Jacobi. But he's a screwball—bad judgment—unreliable—a problem rather than a help."

The Kaczynski Moment dislocates. Suddenly, everyone seems to be living in a dream world. Why are they talking about binge TV and the latest political outrage when we're turning the goddamn atmosphere into a vast tanker of Zyklon B? Was he right? Were we all gelded and put in harnesses without even knowing it? Is this just a simulation of life, not life itself?

People have moments like that under normal conditions, of course. Sigmund Freud wrote a famous essay about them way back in 1929, *Civilization and Its Discontents*. A few unsettled souls will always quit that bank job and sail to Tahiti, and the stoic middle will always suck it up. But Jacobi couldn't accept those options. Staggered by the shock of his Kaczynski Moment but intent on rising to the challenge, he began corresponding with the great man himself, hitchhiked the 644 miles from Chapel Hill to Ann Arbor to read the Kaczynski archives, tracked down his followers all around the world, and collected an impressive (and potentially incriminating) cache of material on ITS along the way. He even published essays about them in an alarmingly terror-friendly print journal named *Atassa*. But his biggest influence was a mysterious Spanish radical theorist known only by the pseudonym he used to translate Kaczynski's manifesto into Spanish, Último Reducto. Recommended by Kaczynski himself, who even supplied an email address, Reducto gave Jacobi a daunting reading list and some editorial advice on his early essays, which inspired another series of TV-movie twists in Jacobi's turbulent life. Frustrated by the limits of his knowledge, he applied to the University of North Carolina, Chapel Hill, to study some more, received a full scholarship and a small stipend, and buckled down for two years of intense scholarship. Then he quit and hit the road again. "I think the homeless are a better model than ecologically minded university students," he told me. "They're already living outside of the structures of society."

Four years into this bizarre pilgrimage, Jacobi is something of an underground figure himself—the ubiquitous, eccentric, freakishly intellectual kid who became the Zelig of ecoextremism. Right now, he's about to skin his first rat. Barefoot and shirtless, with an old wool blanket draped over his shoulders, long sunstreaked hair and gleaming blue eyes, he hurries down a rocky mountain trail toward a stone-age village of wattle-and-daub huts, softening his voice to finish his thought. "Ted was a good start. But Ted is not the endgame."

He stops there. The village ahead is the home of a "primitive skills" school called Wild Roots. Blissfully untainted by modern conveniences like indoor toilets and hot showers, it's also free of charge. It has just three rules, and only one that will get us kicked out. "I don't want to be associated with that name," Wild Roots' de facto leader told us when I mentioned Kaczynski. "I don't want my name associated with that name," he added. "I *really* don't want to be associated with that name."

Jacobi arrives at the open-air workshop, covered by a tin roof, where the dirtiest Americans I've ever seen are learning how to weave cordage from bark, start friction fires, skin animals. The only surprise is the lives they led before: a computer analyst for a military-intelligence contractor, a PhD candidate in engineering, a classical violinist, two schoolteachers, and a rotating cast of college students the older members call the "pre-postapocalypse generation." Before he became the community blacksmith, the engineering student was testing batteries for ecofriendly cars. "It was a fucking hoax," he says now. "It wasn't going to make any difference." At his coal-fired forge, pounding out simple tools with a hammer and anvil, he feels much more useful. "I can't make my own axes yet, but I made most of the handles on those tools, I make all my own punches and chisels. I made an adze. I can make knives."

Freshly killed this morning, five dead rats lie on a pine board. They're for practice before trying to skin larger game. Jacobi bends down for a closer look, selects a rat, ties a string to its twiggy leg, and hangs it from a rafter. He picks up a razor. "You wanna leave the cartilage in the ear," his teacher says. "Then cut just above the white line and you'll get the eyes off."

A few feet away, a young woman who fled an elite women's college in Boston pounds a wooden staff into a bucket to pulverize hemlock bark to make tannin to tan the bear hide she has soaking in the stream—a mixture of mashed hemlock and brain tissue is best, she says, though eggs can substitute if you can't get fresh brain.

Jacobi works the razor carefully. The eyes fall into the dirt.

"I'm surprised you haven't skinned a rat before," I say.

"Yeah, me too," he replies.

He is, after all, the founder of The Wildernist and HunterGatherer, two of the more radical web journals in the personal "rewilding" movement. The moderates at places like ReWild University talk of "rewilding your taste buds" and getting in "rockin' fit shape." "We don't have to demonize our culture or attempt to hide from it," ReWild University's website enthuses. Jacobi has no interest in padding the walls of the cage—as he put it in an essay titled "Taking Rewilding Seriously," "You can't rewild an animal in a zoo."

He's not an idiot; he knows the zoo is pretty much everywhere at this point. He explained this in the philosophical book he wrote at twenty-two, *Repent to the Primitive:* "My focus on the hunter/gatherer is based on a tradition in political philosophy that considers the natural state of man before moving on to an analysis of the civilized state of man. This is the tradition of Hobbes, Rousseau, Locke, Hume, Paine." His plan is to ace his primitive skills, then test living wild for an extended time in the deepest forest he can find.

So why did it take him so long to get out of the zoo?

"I thought sabotage was more important," he says.

But this isn't the place to talk about that—he doesn't want to break Wild Roots' rules. Jacobi goes silent and works his razor down the rat's body, pulling the skin down like a sock.

When he's finished, he leads the way back into the woods, naming the plants: pokeberry, sourwood, rhododendron, dog hobble, tulip poplar, hemlock. The one with orange flowers is a lily that will garnish his dinner tonight. "If you want, I can get some for you," he offers.

Then he returns to the forbidden topic. "I could never do anything like that," he says firmly—unless he could, which is also a possibility. "I don't have any moral qualms with violence," he says. "I would go to jail, but for what?"

For what? The first time I talked to him, he told me he had dreams of being the leader Kaczynski wanted.

"I am being a little evasive," he admits. His other reason for going to college, he says, was to plant the anti-civ seed in the future lawyers and scientists gathered there—"people who will defend you, people who have access to computer networks"—and also, speaking purely speculatively, who could serve as "the material for a terrorist criminal network."

"Did you convince anybody?" I ask.

"I don't know. I always told them not to tell me."

"So you wanted to be the Lenin?"

"Yeah, I wanted to be Lenin."

But let's face it, he says, the revolution's never going to happen. Probably. Maybe. That's why he's heading into the woods. "I want to come out in a few years and be like Jesus," he jokes, "working miracles with plants."

Isn't he doing exactly what Lenin did during his exile in Europe, though? Honing his message, building a network, weighing tactical options, and creating a mystique. Is he practicing "security culture," the activist term for covering your tracks? "Are you hiding the truth? Are you secretly plotting with your hard-core cadre?"

He smiles. "I wouldn't be a very good revolutionary if I told you I was doing that."

At the last minute, Abe Cabrera changed our rendezvous point from a restaurant in New Orleans to an alligator-filled swamp an hour away. This wasn't a surprise. Jacobi had given me Cabrera's email address, identifying him as the North American contact for ITS, which Cabrera immediately denied. His interest in ITS was purely academic, he insisted, an outgrowth of his studies in liberation theology. "However," he added, "to say that I don't have any contact with them may or may not be true."

Now he's leading me into the swamp, literally, talking about an ITS bomb attack on the head of the Department of Physical and Mathematical Sciences at the University of Chile in 2011. "Is that a fair target?" he asks. "For Uncle Ted, it would have been, so I guess that's the standard." He chuckles.

He's short, round, bald, full of nervous energy, wild theories, and awkward tics—if "Terrorist Spokesman" doesn't work out for him, he's a shoo-in for "Mad Scientist in a B-Movie." Giant ferns and carpets of moss appear and disappear as he leads the way into the swamp, where the elephantine roots of cypress trees stand in the eerie stillness of the water like dinosaurs.

He started checking out ITS after he heard some rumors about a new cell starting up in Torreón, his grandparents' birthplace in Mexico, he says, but the group didn't really catch his interest until it changed its name from Individuals Tending Toward the Wild to Wild Reaction. Why? Because healthy animals don't have "tendencies" when they confront an enemy. As one Wild Reaction member put it in the inevitable postattack communiqué, another example of the purple prose poetry that has become the group's signature: "I place the device, and it transforms me into a coyote thirsting for revenge."

Cabrera calls this "radical animism," a phrase that conjures the specter of nature itself rising up in revolt. Somehow that notion wove together all the dizzying twists his life had taken—the years as the child of migrant laborers in the vegetable fields of California's Imperial Valley, his flirtation with "super-duper Marxism" at UC Berkeley, the leap of faith that put him in an "ultraconservative, ultra-Catholic" order, and the loss of faith that surprised him at the birth of his child. "Most people say, 'I held my kid for the first time and I realized God exists.' I held my kid the first time and I said, 'You know what? God is bullshit.'" People were great in small doses but deadly in large ones, even the beautiful little girl cradled in his arms. There were no fundamental ethical values. It all came down to numbers. If that was God's plan, the whole thing was about as spiritually "meaningful as a marshmallow," Cabrera says.

John Jacobi is a big part of this story, he adds. They connected on Facebook after a search for examples of radical animism led him to Hunter-Gatherer. They both contributed to the journal *Atassa*, which was dedicated on the first page to the premise that "civilization should be fought" and that the example of Ted Kaczynski "is what that fighting looks like." In the premier edition, Jacobi made the prudent decision to write in a detached tone. Cabrera's essay bogs down in turgid scholarship before breaking free with a flourish of suspiciously familiar prose poetry: "Ecoextremists believe that this world is garbage. They understand progress as industrial slavery, and they fight like cornered wild animals since they know that there is no escape."

Cabrera weaves in and out of corners like a prisoner looking for an escape route, so it's hard to know why he chose a magazine reporter for his most incendiary confession: "Here's the super-official version I haven't told anybody—I am the unofficial voice-slash-theoretician of ecoextremism. I translated all thirty communiqués. I translated one last night."

Abe Cabrera: Abracadabra.

Yes, he knows this puts him dangerously close to violating the laws against material contributions to terrorism. He read the Patriot Act. That's why he leads a double life, even a triple life. Nobody at work knows, nobody from his past knows, even his wife doesn't know. He certainly doesn't want his kids to know. He doesn't even want to tell them about climate change. Math homework, piano lessons, gymnastics, he's "knee-deep in all that stuff." He punches the clock. "What else am I gonna do? I love my kids," he says. "I hope for their future, even though they have no future."

His mood sinks, reminding me of Jacobi. Shifts in perspective seem to be part of this world. Puma hunted here before the Europeans came, Cabrera says, staring into the swamp. Bears and alligators, too, things that could kill you. The cypress used to be three times as thick. When you look around, you see how much everything has suffered.

But we're not in this mess because of greed or nihilism; we're in it because we love our children so much we made too many of them. And we're just so good at dominating things, all that is left is to lash out in a "wild reaction," Cabrera says. That's why he sympathizes with ITS. "It's like, 'Be the psychopathic destruction you want to see in the world,'" he says, tossing out one last mordant chuckle in place of a good-bye.

Kaczynski is annoyed with me. "*Do not* write me anything more about ITS," he said. "You could get me in trouble that way." He went on: "What is bad about an article like the one I expect you to write is that it may help make the anti-tech movement into another part of the spectacle (along with Trump, the 'metoo movement,' neo-Nazis, antifa, etc.) that keeps people entertained and therefore thoughtless."

ITS, he says, is the very reason he cut Jacobi off. Even after Kaczynski told him the warden was dying for a reason to reduce his contacts with the outside world, the kid kept sending him news about them. He ended his letter to me with a controlled burst of fury. "A hypothesis: ITS is instigated by some country's security services—probably Mexico. Their real task is to spread hopelessness, because where there is no hope there is no serious resistance."

Wait . . . Ted Kaczynski is hopeful? The Ted Kaczynski who wants to destroy civilization? The idea seems ridiculous right up to the moment it spins around and becomes reasonable. What better evidence could you find than the unceasing stream of tactical and strategic advice that he's sent from his prison cell for almost twenty years, after all. He's hopeful that civilization can be taken down in time to save some of the planet. I guess I just couldn't imagine how anyone could ever manage to rally a group of ecorevolutionaries large enough to do the job.

"If you've read my *Anti-Tech Revolution*, then you haven't understood it," he scolds. "All you have to do is disable some key components of the system so that the whole thing collapses." I do remember the "small core of deeply committed people" and "Hit Where It Hurts," but it's still hard to fathom. "How long does it take to do that?" Kaczynski demands. "A year? A month? A week?"

On paper, Deep Green Resistance meets most of his requirements. The original core group spent five years holding conferences and private meetings to hone its message and build consensus, then publicized it effectively with its book, which speculates about tactical alternatives to stop the "planet from burning to a cinder": "If selective disruption doesn't work soon enough, some resisters may conclude that all-out disruption is needed" and launch "coordinated actions on a large scale" against key targets. DGR now has as many as two hundred thousand members, according to the group's cofounder—a soft-spoken thirty-year-old named Max Wilbert—who could shave off his Mephistophelian goatee and disappear into any crowd. Two hundred thousand may not sound like much when Beyoncé has one million–plus Instagram followers, but it's not shabby in a world where lovers cry out pseudonyms during sex. And Fidel had only nineteen in the jungles of Cuba, as Kaczynski likes to point out.

Jacobi says DGR was hobbled by a doctrinal war over "TERFS," an acronym I had to look up—it's short for "trans-exclusionary radical feminists"—so this summer they're rallying the troops with a crash course in "resistance training" at a private retreat outside Yellowstone National Park in Montana. "This training is aimed at activists who are tired of ineffective actions," the promotional flyer says. "Topics will include hard and soft blockades, hit-and-run tactics, police interactions, legal repercussions, operational security, terrain advantages and more."

At the Avis counter at the Bozeman airport, my phone dings. It's an email from the organizers of the event, saying a guy named Matt needs a ride. I find him standing by the curb. He's in his early thirties, dressed in conventional clothes, short hair, no visible tattoos, the kind of person you'd send to check out a visitor from the media. When we get on the road and have a chance to talk, he says he's a middle-school social-studies teacher. He's sympathetic to the urge to escalate, but he'd prefer to destroy civilization by nonviolent means, possibly by "decoupling" from the modern world, town by town and state by state.

But if that's true, why is he here?

"See for yourself," he said.

We reach the camp in the late afternoon and set up our tents next to a big yurt. A mountain rises behind us, another mountain stands ahead; a narrow lake fills the canyon between them as the famous Big Sky, blushing at the advances of the night, justifies its association with the sublime. "Nature is the only place where you feel awe," Jacobi told me after the leaves rustled at Wild Roots, and right now it feels true.

An hour later, the group gathers in the yurt outfitted with a plywood floor, sofas, and folding chairs: one student activist from UC Irvine, two Native American veterans of the Standing Rock pipeline protests, three radical lawyers, a shy working-class kid from Mississippi, a former abortion-clinic volunteer, and a few people who didn't want to be identified or quoted in any way. The session starts with a warning about loose lips and a lecture on DGR's "nonnegotiable guidelines" for men—hold back, listen, agree or disagree respectfully, avoid male-centered words, and follow the lead of women.

By that time, I'd already committed my first microaggression. The cook asked why I was standing in the kitchen doorway, and I answered, "Just supervising." Her sex had nothing to do with it, I swear—I was waiting to wash my hands and, frankly, her question seemed a bit hostile. But the woman who followed me out the door to dress me down said that refusing to accept her criticism was another microaggression.

The first speaker turns the mood around. His name is Sakej Ward, and he did a tour in Afghanistan with the US Joint Airborne and a few years in the Canadian military. He's also a full-blooded member of the Wolf Clan of British Columbia and the Mi'kmaq of northern Maine with two degrees in political science, impressive muscles bulging through a T-shirt from some karate club, and one of those flat, wide Mohawks you see on outlaw bikers. Unfortunately, he put his entire presentation off the record, so all I can tell you is that the theme was Native American warrior societies. Later he tells me the societies died out with the buffalo and the open range. They revived sporadically in the last quarter of the twentieth century, but returned in earnest at events like Standing Rock. "It's a question of 'Are they there yet?' We've been fighting this war for five hundred years. But climate change is creating an atmosphere where it can happen."

For the next two days, we get training in computer security and old activist techniques like using "lockboxes" to chain yourself to bulldozers and fences—given almost apologetically, like a class in 1950s home cooking. In another session, Ward takes us to a field and lines us up single file. Imagine you're on a military patrol, he says, turning his back and holding his left hand out to the side, elbow at ninety degrees and palm forward. "Freeze!" he barks.

We freeze.

"That's the best way to conceal yourself from the enemy," he tells us. He runs through basic Army-patrol semiotics. For "enemy," you make a pistol with your hand and turn it thumbs-down. "Danger area" is a diagonal slash. After showing us a dozen signs, he stops. "Why am I making all the signs with my left hand?"

No one knows.

He turns around to face us with his finger pointed down the barrel of an invisible gun. "Because you always have to have a finger in control of your weapon," he says.

The trainees are pumped afterward. "You can take out transformers with a .50 caliber," one man says.

"But you don't just want to do one," says another. "You want four-man teams taking out ten transformers. That would bring the whole system to a halt."

Kaczynski would be fairly pleased with this so far, I think. Ward is certainly a plausible contender for the Lenin role. Wilbert might be too. "We talk about 'cascading catastrophic effects,'" he tells us in one of the last yurt meetings, summing up DGR's grand strategy. "A large percent of the nation's oil supply is processed in a facility in Louisiana, for example. If that was taken down, it would have cascading effects all over the world."

But then the DGR women called us together for a lecture on patriarchy, which has to be destroyed at the same time as civilization. Also, men who voluntarily assume gendered aspects of female identity should never be allowed in female-sovereign spaces—and don't call them terfs unless you want a speech on microaggression.

Matt listens from the fringes in a hoodie and mirrored glasses, looking exactly like the famous police sketch of the Unabomber. I'm pretty sure he's trolling them. Maybe he's remembering the same Kaczynski quote I am: "Take measures to exclude all leftists, as well as the assorted neurotics, lazies, incompetents, charlatans, and persons deficient in self-control who are drawn to resistance movements in America today."

At the farewell dinner, one of the more mysterious trainees finally speaks up. With long, wild hair, a floppy wilderness hat, pants tucked into waterproof boots, a wary expression, and an actual hermit's cabin in Montana, he projects the anti-civ vibe with impressive authenticity. He was involved in some risky stuff during the Cove Mallard logging protests in Idaho in the mid-1990s, he says, but he retreated after the FBI brought him in for questioning. Lately, though, he's been getting the feeling that things are starting to change, and now he's sure of it. "I've been in a coma for twenty years," he says. "I want to thank you guys for being here when I woke up." One of the radical lawyers wraps up with a lyrical tribute to the leaders of Ireland's legendary 1916 rebellion. He waxes about Thomas MacDonagh, the schoolteacher who led the Dublin brigade and whistled as he was led to the firing squad.

On the drive back to the airport, I ask Matt if he's really a middle-school teacher. He answers with a question: What is your real interest in this thing?

I mention John Jacobi. "I know him," he says. "We've traded a few emails."

Of course he does. He's another serious young man with gears turning behind his eyes.

"Can you imagine actually doing something like that?" I ask.

"Well," he answers, drawing out the pause, "Thomas MacDonagh was a schoolteacher."

The next time I talk to John Jacobi, he's back in Chapel Hill living with a friend and feeling shaky. Things were getting strange at Wild Roots, he says—nobody could cooperate, there were personal conflicts. And, well, there was an incident with molly. It's been a hard four years. First he lost Jesus and anarchy. Then Kaczynski and Último Reducto dumped him, which was really painful, though he understood why. "I've been unreliable," he says woefully. To make matters worse, an ITS member called Los Hijos del Mencho denounced him by name online: The trouble with Jacobi was his "reluctance to support indiscriminate attacks" because of his sentimental attachment to humanity.

Jacobi is considering the possibility that his troubled past may have affected his judgment. He still believes in the revolution, he says, but he's not sure what he'd do if somebody gave him a magic bottle of Civ-Away. He'd probably use it. Or maybe not.

I check in a couple of weeks later. He's working in a fish store and thinking of going back to school. Maybe he can get a job in forest conservation. He'd like to have a kid someday.

He brings up Paul Kingsnorth, the "recovering environmentalist" who got rattled by Kaczynski's manifesto in 2012. Kingsnorth's answer to our global existential crisis was mourning, reflection, and the search for "the hope beyond hope." The group he co-founded to help people with that task, a mixture of therapy group and think tank called Dark Mountain, now has more than fifty chapters worldwide. "I'm coming to terms with the fact that it might very well be true that there's not much you can do," Jacobi says, "but I'm having a real hard time just letting go with a hopeless sigh."

In his Kaczynski essay, Kingsnorth, who has since moved to Ireland to homeschool his kids and write novels, put his finger on the problem. It was the hidden side effect of the Kaczynski Moment: paralysis. "I am still embedded, at least partly because I can't work out where to jump, or what to land on, or whether you can ever get away by jumping, or simply because I'm frightened to close my eyes and walk over the edge." To the people who end up in that suspended state now and then, lying in bed at four in the morning imagining the worst, here's Kingsnorth's advice: "You can't think about it every day. I don't. You'll go mad!"

It's winter now and Jacobi's back on the road, sleeping in bushes and scavenging for food, looking for his place to land. Sometimes I wonder if he makes these journeys into the forest because of the way his mother ended her life—maybe he's searching for the wild beasts and ministering angels she heard when he fell to his knees and spoke the language of God. Psychologists call that magical thinking. Medication and counseling are more effective treatments for trauma, they say. But maybe the dream of magic is the magic, the dream that makes the dream come true, and maybe grief is a gift too, a check on our human arrogance. Doesn't every crisis summon the healers it needs?

In the poems Jacobi wrote after his mother hanged herself, she turned into a tree and sprouted leaves.

PERMISSIONS

ABOUT THE AUTHOR

John H. Richardson was born in Washington, D.C., in 1954. He grew up in Athens, Manila, Saigon, Washington, Seoul, Honolulu, and Los Angeles. He is a graduate of the University of Southern California '77 and Columbia University '82. His writing has appeared in the *Albuquerque Tribune*, *The Los Angeles Daily News*, *Premiere*, *New York*, and *Esquire*. He has taught at Columbia University, the University of New Mexico, and Purchase College. *Sing Sing Follies* is his fifth book.

ABOUT THE PUBLISHER

The Sager Group was founded in 1984. In 2012 it was chartered as a multimedia content brand, with the intent of empowering those who create art—an umbrella beneath which makers can pursue, and profit from, their craft directly, without gatekeepers. TSG publishes books; ministers to artists and provides modest grants; and produces documentary, feature, and commercial films. By harnessing the means of production, The Sager Group helps artists help themselves. For more information, please see TheSagerGroup.net.

Artifex Te Adiuva

Made in United States
North Haven, CT
19 February 2025

66046997R00109